THE THOUGHT IS THE CAUSE OF IT ALL

JOHHNNY X WILLIAMSON

Copyright © 2014 Johnny X. Williamson

All rights reserved.

ISBN: **10: 0985759240**
ISBN-13: **978-0985759247**

DEDICATION

The Thoughts in "The Cause of It All" are for people who are thinkers, and for those who would like to learn how to think more positive and critically. The Inspiration and Motivation to write this book came from The Honorable Minister Louis Farrakhan, my spiritual leader and teacher......

All rights reserved. No part of this publication may be used or reproduced in any manner whatsoever without the written permission of the Author and/or the Publisher. Printed in the United States of America. To contact the Publisher, email us at Vanguard Educational Services Academic Press, vanguardedsrv@gmail.com. PO Box 77875 Greensboro, NC 27417

CONTENTS

Acknowledgements

Foreword 7

Introduction 14

1 The Law and Principal of Thought 17
2 Open and Closed Consciousness (Negative and Positive) 24
3 Your Real Self: The Power of the Conscious Mind 34
4 Your Greater Self: Waking Up the Subconscious Mind 37
5 Ideas and Reality: Where Do They Come From? 43
6 The Powerful Emotion of Fear: It Cannot Control You 53
7 Big Faith: Do You Have Any? 57
8 Success: Where and How To Find It 68
9 Go Get Your Share: Abundance and More Abundance 75
10 Man Has Always Had the Power To Do For Self 86
11 Control Yourself: Desire Feeds the Will 94
12 The Ruts of Life 106
13 Who Are You: Find Your True Self 112
14 Tune In and Go Make Yourself Great 117
15 Be Still: The Principal of Silence 122
16 The Invisible Design: The Pattern of Now 125
17 Reality: Caution and Reflection 128
18 The Time Factor: What Must Be Done Now 131
19 Dr Johnny X Menu for Success 136
20 The Internal Enemy: Man and Woman are on the Brink of Destruction 142
Epilogue: Original Quotations 150

ACKNOWLEDGMENTS

First, I would like to thank the Honorable Minister Louis Farrakhan for providing me with the external motivation to prepare this book. Although I was isolated from the outside world, the Minister gave me the desire and will-power to complete the book, when he told me that we could overcome any difficulty.

I also give thanks to Mr. Larry Floyd for assisting me with the pre-editing and typing of the manuscript. I certainly thank my wife, Mrs. Equilla Allen Williamson for listening to me as I discussed the concepts and purpose of the book. She was very inspirational.

Also, thanks are extended to my daughter Sabrina. She kept the fire burning while I was composing the last chapters of the book. I am most grateful for that – thank you.

Lastly, I want to thank Dr. Toni Muhammad, for her tireless editing of the final draft into a master piece.

FOREWORD

It was the title that first caught my eye. "The Thought is the Cause of It All," a fascinating subject that has held my attention for years.

I read the first page of Johnny X Williamson's powerful book and its references to "the inner workings of the human mind," and I knew I had stumbled upon a masterpiece of supreme wisdom unknown to the average person.

It is a given that most people, for the most part, are taught to think a certain way, to act a certain way and to behave a certain way. We are trained and conditioned to conform, to observe the status quo, to fit in, and to go-along in order-to-get along.

It has been said that every great accomplishment and every dramatic failure was first made in the mind. Thus, the thoughts we hold in our minds, good or bad, create our reality. We are, in fact, made or unmade by our thoughts. The British writer James Allen, best known for his small book, "As a Man Thinketh," wrote, "All that a man becomes or fails to become is directly related to his thoughts. A man can rise no higher than his thoughts."

No truer words have ever been spoken because a man's behavior is a direct reflection of his most dominating thoughts. Williamson's expert and penetrating analysis of human consciousness makes it crystal clear that, bad thoughts lead to bad deeds and bad actions, while good thoughts lead to good deeds, good examples and good results.

It is good to be aware of a well known fact – every thought held in the mind and every thought released from the mind, represents tiny particles of vibratory energy or what may be classified as living matter, a form of divine energy which can be neither be created or destroyed. Still, most people are completely unaware that thoughts are things, exceedingly powerful things.

This book also offers a framework for the notion that anything that stays on the mind, "*long enough and strong enough,*" sooner or later, will show up in our life. Good or bad, you get to keep whatsoever you can *keep on your mind*!

Now, it doesn't matter whether the stuff percolating in your mind is good or bad, real or imaginary, it's just a matter of time before the *real stuff* shows up in *real time* in your life. Remember the prophetic words of the prophet Job, "…that which I greatly feared has come upon me."

If you have a feeling, for example, that you are going to be laid off from your job, please know that you are, consciously or unconsciously, "feeding that feeling." And eventually, you will get laid off!

There's no getting around it, the dominating thoughts on the mind eventually becomes the dominating reality. Again, be aware, that you get to keep whatever you are holding in your mind. It's just that simple and also just that complicated.

Complicated because most people cannot keep what they want on their mind long enough and strong enough for manifestation to take place. The process is further complicated by the mere fact that many simply (1) *don't know what they really want*, and (2) do not want it *"hard enough."*

Then, too, some people are too quick to settle for less; many, if not the majority, live far below their designated potential. They tend to aim for mediocrity instead of greatness; simplicity instead of excellence, ordinary instead of extraordinary. A "thank God for this little bit," mentality is the rule, rather than the exception.

It sounds harsh, and probably goes against everything you've been taught, but your station in life is largely self-determined. Your reality, your success or failure in other words is self-created.

In short, it is from our thoughts that results, good or bad, are created. Your life, therefore, is a reflection of your innermost thoughts. So, "86," watching other people, direct your attention to watching your own thoughts.

Some people thought he was crazy or a bit immature when he crowned himself with the title, "I AM the greatest," but Muhammad Ali became what he thought he could become, and held fast to that thought. He became great because he knew what he wanted.

Carter G. Woodson, the second black man to earn a Ph.D. from Harvard, became the father of Black History Month because he also knew what he wanted. His thinking was very clear, direct and precise. So clear, in fact, that he would go on to author the breakthrough classic, "The Mis-Education of the Negro," a must-read for anyone in need of self-validation. It was Dr. Woodson's classic work that empowered me to rediscover my real self. This great work fertilized my mind with new insights, new possibilities, and certain truths that had long been hidden from me.

I did not know I had been, "mis-educated," until Dr. Woodson told me so. That book lit a fire in my imagination. It made me conscious about life, about my manhood, about my blackness. Precisely, *I want for my brothers and sisters what I want for myself*! I want joy, peace of mind, some good love and some good health for our entire community. I also want us to have some good money, plenty of it, so that we can be a blessing to others. I want us to learn how to sell and how to provide our own employment. Be a job-maker, not a job-taker! Learn to do for self!

I want us to be good examples for our children and for the beautiful ones who are not yet born. I want our families to be whole again, to show and give love again.

I want us to be upright, righteous seekers of knowledge, wisdom, respect and admiration so that our light will shine brighter and longer, even in our darkest hours.

I want us to overrule the emotions o fear, doubt and worry by replacing them with hope, faith, charity, and love. I want to never be ashamed to bend my knees and pray to a power greater than myself and to understand with great clarity that, "to whom much is given, much is required!"

I want to practice gratitude and forgiveness even when it hurts me to do so. I don't know everything, but there is one thing I am crystal clear about:

I know what I don't want! So I will keep my mind on what I really do want…a reality Williamson has already fixed in our minds by teaching us that "the thought is the cause of it all." Indeed it is!

- John Raye
Life/Wellness/Business Coach
Kernersville, NC
September, 2013

INTRODUCTION

There was a garage door to which I found no key;
There was a type of darkness which I could not see;
Then to the Most High that I cried.
"What stars has destiny to guide,
Where humans are struggling in the dark."
Then a wee small voice replied
"To know thyself is the key."

— Johnny X Williamson

Since the Genesis of human creation and through all the succeeding ages, mankind has believed that there is a mighty power that is invisible that dictates and governs the universe, and man has tried to understand that force. In all the great wonders of the world, whether in China, mysterious India, or under the shadows of the Sphinx, there are men of knowledge, wisdom and scholarship who have tried to lift the veil that shrouds the mysteries of life, and each race and generation has made their quest for the Holy Grail.

All over the globe, in every country, we have discovered and are still discovering foot prints of each stage of past civilization, while time maintains a glorious record of man's progressive climb toward truth and liberation.

While prehistoric man was amazed by the phenomena of the sun, moon and stars, the mystery of life and the tragedy of death, they still created a basic system of deities to whose mighty power was attributed things not understood. But as we trace mankind down through the ages, we find his life gradually changed to match his improved mentality, and today we sit on the thresholds of those by-gone centuries and the intellectual masters of all ages.

Today, more than ever before, we have tendencies to ask many questions concerning the meaning of life. From the hard work of the few, we have arrived at the present civilization, and because we are wise we cannot be satisfied with anything other than the truth. We are at a crucial hour when we must ask. **WHY, HOW**, and **WHAT IF!** The time for individual development has come. We must seek and discover the "whys and wherefores **OF ALL THAT AMAZES AND BAFFLES US IN THE UNKNOWN SCHEME OF LIFE AND NATURE.** Each of us must find our place in this complex cosmic order, and then come to the realization what the true meaning of life is**. WE MUST DISCOVER THE KEY TO OUR DESTINY.**

- Johnny X Williamson
Winston-Salem, NC
September, 2013

CHAPTER ONE
The Law and Principles of Thought

> *All that we imagine or interpret,*
> *Comes from a single thought.*
> *When you think, critically or simple,*
> *Those thoughts are only new to you*
> *Because they can be as old as the universe,*
> *Or they can be as new as a newborn baby.*
> *Thought is indeed the cause of it all.*
> — Johnny X Williamson

Thinking is probably the most powerful force human beings have in their arsenals. **THINKING IS THE ULTIMATE BUSINESS OF LIFE. THINKING IS THE TRUE BUSINESS OF LIFE.** Thinking is the process that makes the world turn, and thinkers rule the world. They always have, and they always will.

It is very true, that all people think, but unfortunately, few of us think creatively and constructively or recognize that "THOUGHT" is a divine creative force, one that has no beginning or end. There is no real achievement that exists, whether in business, literature, philosophy, or science, that has not found its origin and fullest expression through the mental efforts of the world's leaders, thinkers and motivators. And guess what, the outstanding thinkers of today, will become the future leaders of tomorrow. **THE THOUGHT IS THE CAUSE OF IT ALL.**

I have many personal friends and family members all over the world, including those in America. We live in the same world, but we are completely different as much as the sun is to the moon. One gives light and the older reflects light. Our thought processes are the cause of everything. Some people are sick, others are strong and healthy; some of us fail while others are extremely successful, wonder why? There are those who are really miserable, and others are joyfully happy. We often blame bad luck on our fellow man, and take the credit for all the good that comes our way. But, in reality, the difference is in ourselves. We are the products of traditional beliefs and habits of thought. For instance, if we start a race at the same time, my chances of completing the race are just as good as yours. Maybe, I will beat you to the finish line, that's only because maybe I am just a little bit faster than you. But regardless of what you or my situation or conduct is, the cause of our situations and condition has roots. You see, our problems most often times start in our minds. The cause had to find a place in our consciousness before it could develop into an expression. That's why I believe that we can change ourselves, recreate ourselves, improve our conditions, control the environment, and yes, we can become masters of our own destiny. This isn't a writer's theory; this is an actual fact, based on positive knowledge. The principle is, **EVERYTHING THAT WE NEED IS ON THE INSIDE OF US**.

This is for all of us that still believe and rely on luck and chance: wake-up! Our lives are absolutely governed and controlled by laws; by actual, immutable principles that never change. There is never a moment when some type of law if <u>inoperable</u>. These laws are in all places.

They are mighty, silent laws that affect and underlie every human action; laws that are not racist, partial, and are no respecter of person(s). When you see Don King or Donald Trump doing and making big things happen, or when they take business to a higher level, they are under the law of success. Once Mr. Trump said, "**WHEN I'M IN MY ZONE, I FEEL THAT I CAN'T LOSE.**" Therefore, I make decisions based on this type of winning attitude. They have discovered how to go deep down within their minds to bring out what is necessary to plan, build, and duplicate it again and again. **THE LAW OF THOUGHT IS AMAZING.**

When we see flowers growing, the snowflakes falling, these are only testaments of some great law in affect. We may not know exactly what causes the sun, moon, stars and tides of the sea to work, but we all would probably admit that there is some type of great force causing them to work as they do, would you agree? It is a law that makes the universe stay on course and in harmony. Here is another way to understand it; everything and everybody must submit to a law. **THE THOUGHT IS THE CAUSE OF IT ALL**! There is but one power source, one principle, **ONE CAUSE**. And yes, the thought is its father and mother. We must remember that these laws will work for us or against us. Against us when we work against the natural principles; it works when the divine principles of the law, we will be able to bring that law under our power-control-zone, thereby making the law subservient to us. **THE LAW WILL WORK THROUGH US AND FOR US**.

It is natural for humans to be whole and healthy in mind, body and soul, and for them to do well in all walks of life. When we learn this powerful truth and (get and) stay in accordance with this law, our health and prosperity will germinate naturally and abundantly. Most people, if not all, believe in having plenty of everything on hand. Illness and health, wealth and poverty are all connected and interwoven in this divine providence.

But those of us, though few in number, know that life, health and abundance are controlled by laws of the universe. And guess what? **THOUGHT IS THE ONLY PRINCIPLE (LAW) BY WHICH WE ARE CONNECTED TO THINGS WE RELATE TO**

DESIRE, WANT, AND NEED. Therefore, whatever it is that we want in life, all we have to do is to **"THINK IT INTO REALITY"** because **"THOUGHT IS THE CAUSE OF IT ALL."**

The mind and brain aren't the same. The Brain is a transmitter, and the Mind is a "THINK TANK." **The mind is the thinker of the body.** Everything else has its origination and beginning in the MIND, everything! Thought is only the Mind at work, doing what it is made to do. And since thought is creative, it is capable of creating shape, form, and anything that the mind can conceive, that same mind can achieve it. Some great person once said that **MIND IS OVER MATTER.** I am certainly in agreement with that conclusion.

Can you remember a time when you had a wonderful thought, and all of a sudden it seemed to disappear? What happened to it? Well, a Thought is only a vibration, and if it is to evolve, it must make the connection to what I call, '**THE THINKING CELL."** This cell will take a thought in its original form, and shape it into its desired form. After this **THINKING**

CELLS makes the proper contact with the **MOVING AND DOING CELLS**, which I call the **ACTION or MATURITY CELL**. Now, at this moment, the body is ready to take orders from the powerful force that is called **THOUGHT**.

CHAPTER TWO
Open and Closed Consciousness

Our negatives and positives are
Wrapped-up in our Soul's DNA.
The remedy for self-help is
Buried within our minds.
- Johnny X Williamson

It is important that the readers of this book become fully aware of what consciousness really means. Although we may sometimes be somewhat knowledgeable of a topic, it still may not be a part of our sub-consciousness. To illustrate: I once was a student at a local barber's college, and the teacher would normally place on the black board all types of hair styles and designs. She would explain, and then explain some more. And certainly some of us thought that we had mastered those designs, but when test time came, it was apparent that we did not fully understand what we thought we understood. So, if we deal with hind sight, we must ask this question, "Did we really and truly understand the essence of the teacher's illustrations? **I THINK NOT.**

But, if we had really studied the designs, and concentrated on them for a while, then perhaps, it would have stayed with us. And maybe we would have grasped and understood the information. The mind is powerful when used properly. Can you see the point? There is a big difference in knowing and thinking that you know. It is very possible for us to intellectually perceive something without it becoming a part of our inner consciousness.   I   call   this   the   **"CLOSED CONSCIOUSNESS."**

So that is why it is critically important for us to study these lessons with intense passion and desire for correct view. Because when we **"QUICK READ"** we will normally miss the hidden meaning of what we are reading. Like I said, when we go over information quickly, at best we will only be able to remember the words, but we will slide right on by the real meaning. And when we read information quickly, absent of critical thought, most times it will evade the department in the mind that it needs to go – **the "STORE HOUSE"** of facts and information, the sub-conscious. I am suggesting that you and I, even if we already know this, find ways to re-read material over at least twice. Quick reading is too risky, and will not do us any good. I would like you and me to take these lessons into the **"SILENCE WITHIN US"** until they connect to our soul, spirit, and consciousness, which I call the **"SECRET CHAMBER OF KNOWLEDGE."**

Most people think that to concentrate takes a lot of effort, but quite the contrary is true. Can you remember the time when you lost yourself in a wonderful and powerful novel, you got so into the book until all of your surroundings totally obliterated? That's real concentration, and we have the power to train ourselves to meditate so that we can focus our whole selves on whatever we are involved with. **HAVE YOU EVER**

TRIED MEDITATION? If you have, goo, if not you should try it. Let's try it together. Ok, find a **SILENT SPOT**. Now, empty your mind, that's right, I said to empty it. You can do this by dumping all of the stuff that is lodged in your mind, whether good or bad, get rid of it. Now you are ready, all you have to do is tell your mind **to BE EMPTY**. In other words, there isn't anything that you and I cannot do if we focus our minds on the proper **THOUGHTS**. Remember, the mind's assignment is only to think. Well, it's about time we let it do its job.

As we proceed through the process of meditation, our mind will find a way to lock itself into a single thought mode or channel. The mind has the capability to isolate thoughts into single categories. We have the **POWER** to subdue our minds by controlling our thoughts. The mind is infinite and powerful. From this day forward, I want you to find **this SILENT SPOT** and take a few minutes to turn our **THOUGHTS** within, so that we can take a realistic inventory of ourselves, because this is probably the only way we can deal with truth and actual facts.

While you are in this silent spot, you probably will not discover any monumental miracles, but you certainly will discover powerful emotions that you did not know existed. The purpose of this silent spot is to provide a certain type of stillness that closes out all distractions. Let's call this the **IMPRISONMENT OF THE MIND.** In this mode, you will find the place where you can rest your mind and body thereby accessing the power to control and direct your thoughts into a perfect operational channel. Engaging in this process will be of great benefit to you.

We truly must learn how to control our thoughts. Most people find it difficult to think consistently on one subject for any length of time. Our minds' seems to want to jump from topic to topic; doing otherwise seems impossible for normal human beings. Unless you have extensive training in mind control, you will not be able to think multiple thoughts at the same time. I repeat, it is very hard to train your mind in that manner, since it usually rejects outside influences that tell it how to reason. After all, that is the mind's original function.

I believe we should work on methods to bring our thoughts back to their primary function which is to serve, not lead. Sometimes our thoughts want to play **BOSS,** but when we work at keeping them in check we can bring them back in line quickly. It is critical that we do so, because thoughts can become dangerous when they are allowed to run loose.

If we can learn how to embrace a single thought for 15 to 30 minutes, we immediately become mentally powerful. Most people will find these points on meditation difficult or maybe even impossible while others may say that they're easy. Regardless of your personal opinion, they have great potential. We have to come to the conclusion that our thoughts must be controlled by us. That is the key. We can develop this with a sincere effort.

I strongly believe that if there is to be any degree of efficiency and harmony, it is absolutely necessary that we obtain control of both our physical and mental selves. The lack of harmony in the work place, in schools and in our communities is directly linked to control. When there is a lack of control, chaos and madness reign. I remember getting involved with a highly structured group whose members thought they "lived, ate, and slept discipline." And for a very long time after becoming a part of this very tight organization, I found myself being made to obey the rules. In the past, I had serious problems with self-control, and of course, they were determined to make me learn discipline, forced or otherwise. But, in the end, I not only learned discipline, I also learned **SELF CONTROL.** **THE THOUGHT IS THE CAUSE OF IT ALL.**

A great leader once said: **"TO KNOW IS POWERFUL, BUT TO BECOME SELF-DISCIPLINED IS THE BEGINNING OF TRUE GREATNESS."** What are some of the benefits of self-control? When we learn self-control, we place ourselves in a powerful position to think constructively, and critically. In doing so, we gain a sense of mastery over our thought processes which opens our minds and prepares us to "elevate our conscious to operate on a higher level," and think in a more harmonious fashion. Then we will be able to go into that private spot mentioned previously where we can find our true selves.

If we are to begin developing **our THOUGHTS**, we must find a way to enter this mental room. This is what the masters and scribes meant when they said, **"GO INTO THINE INNER CHAMBER AND SHUT THE DOOR. PRAY TO THE FATHER IN SECRET AND HIS HEARING IN SECRET WILL REWARD YOU OPENLY."** Now, your thought processes can develop. Can you feel them coming alive?

Think and grow rich, but rich in what? Reality is real therefore, **THOUGHT IS THE ONLY REAL REALITY**. Whatever condition we are in, it represents the manifestation of the quality of our thinking. It is widely taught that everything eventually changes which means that thought will ultimately change, as well. One great leader noted that the conditions of a people cannot change until they change their minds. In essence this means that we must learn how to think in a way that shifts our conditions into our desired goal.

People, regardless of their age, are total slaves to what I call, **"THE SERVANTS OF NON-THINKING"** and their master is <u>Low Self-Esteem.</u>

I can remember a time when I was one of those people who thought that if I just did the right type of planning whatever I engaged myself in would instantly become a success. Boy was I ever off target with those thoughts. When I started to enter and embrace the evolutionary process of discovering my true self, then and there **I FOUND THE SECRETS OF SUCCESS** or what I call the **<u>TRAY CONCEPT</u>**. The tray concept works like this. All of us have certain gifts that come directly from God. You see, a gift is not a learned behavior, it's a gift. If we learn to make these unique gifts work for us and allow them to manifest themselves, then we'll be rewarded with the ability to tap into the hidden but powerful gift of THOUGHT. Ok, let us give an example of the **<u>TRAY CONCEPT</u>**. Whatever we have on our personal plates **(OUR BRAIN POWER and SKILL SET),** we can work those traits to achieve a level of success. And if we learn how to add more to our plate while keeping our tray balanced then we simultaneously add to our chances of becoming even more successful. **<u>THE THOUGHT IS THE CAUSE OF IT ALL.</u>**

For example, most of us believe that when we start to think positive that exercise alone will motivate us. Just imagine us being able to think on an idea so extensively that it becomes a part of our **MIND.** Well, we can. But first, I strongly suggest that we consciously avoid all negative ideas, unhealthy thoughts, self-pity, finger-pointing and blaming the other person. Then we can **<u>BUILD-UP OUR THOUGHT PROCESSES</u>** using **our <u>THOUGHTS AS GUIDES</u>**.

CHAPTER THREE
The Power of the Conscious Mind

When you think that you will lose, you will;
You cannot win when you think not to dare.
If you are driven to win, but you think you can't,
It's almost a certainty that you won't.
You and I lost because we thought that we would;
Anything that we desire or need is in the world.
Success begins with a human determination and WILL;
It's all in how we think.
- Johnny X Williamson

When God created us, he made us **"POTENTIALLY COMPLETE."** Each of us is endowed with two aspects of the mind, conscious and subconscious. As was said earlier, the **MIND and BRAIN** are vastly different. The conscious mind governs our ability to perceive, reason, judge, and reject. Under its power, we gain awareness of our gift of thought and our ability to know, to even will, and make individual chooses. The conscious mind is so powerful that it directs how we respond to smell, sight, sound, taste, and feeling. So, if we find ourselves not able to deal with our emotions, we must then resume command and get in touch with our conscious mind. Human beings are endowed with the ability and power to become **GOD-LIKE**; they can become like unto a Serpent or Snake. If we desire to become great, we must first think thoughts of greatness since **THOUGHT IS POWER.**

Now, what did I mean when I said that God made US, man and woman, **POTENTIALLY COMPLETE?** We all started from a low position, and if the process works correctly, we all will evolve into a higher position in life. Of course there are instances when the physical life is cut short because of some malfunction which doctors refer to as the abortive process. When we understand how the mind works, then we have the potential to unplug the hidden power base that each of us possess. But first let's get busy at finding our true self.

We must connect with this **ABSTRACT POWER**, what I call the **"SUPREME RULER OF OUR MENTAL WORLD."** Wouldn't it be nice if we could place the reality of success in our view? Well, we can. When we learn that the power of thought is the most potent live energy in the world, then and only then will we be able to overcome our fear and defeat failure. If success has power, then the enemy of success, failure, also has powerful energies. Success is calling us; what are we waiting on? We were born to win, but prosperity and success waits for NO ONE.

Can you see yourself winning? If you do, that's great because you can accomplish anything that your mind guides you to. Rise and shine, dust yourself off, and start THINKING. You don't have to be great to get started but you'll never become great if you don't. Just take the first step.

CHAPTER FOUR
Waking Up the Subconscious Mind

Men and Women of greatness were once like us.
Those who are so-called experts today were lost yesterday.
They once fumbled and grouped on life's way.
They were fearful of themselves, and thought by Magic was men's Greatness wrought.
They feared to try what they did not know how to do,
And they did not know that they possessed success...
                                        - Johnny X Williamson

The subconscious mind is the master and presides over all the body's **"INVOLUNTARY PROCESSES."** That sounds good intellectually, but what does it really mean? In other words, the subconscious mind dictates to the digestive system, it assimilates, eliminates, governs the beating of the heart, controls the circulation of the blood, it even manufactures the various glandular secretions. This section of the brain is so powerful that it occupies all of the new cells that are born in the body. It's bad, super bad. So, if we program our minds to procrastinate, it will certainly follow our instructions. When we lose or experience failure, most often, it's because we unknowingly convinced our subconscious mind that a negative outcome is what we expect.

I believe that **POSITIVE THINKING BUILDS WITHIN THE BODY CELLS THAT WILL ACT POSITIVE**. That's my personal view although I cannot prove it. I'm not a doctor, at least not yet.

We can change the way we think and in the process renew our cells, "feeding them so that they act as we desire them to and produce positive actions." If we want to think smart and think positively, we must learn to draw from the subconscious. After all, that's where the storehouse of all memory resides. The subconscious is the Chamber of Habits and Instinct; it is where the mothers of emotion resides, and guess what, it works automatically. I know, you're probably saying that it sounds too easy, and believe me, it is also very practical.

We can do it by finding the secret chamber or silent spot and going within ourselves; that's the place where all the answers are.

Is there anything in your storehouse **(SUBCONSCIOUS MIND)** that is powerful enough to extract so that you and I can pull it out? Such as aspects of our inner being that can benefit our condition, and make our lives better. If there is anything positive there, we can and must pull it out **NOW.** We must always keep in mind that the subconscious cannot think, reason, make judgment, or reject. It just does its job which is to take in and record information. The **MIND** does the thinking. The mind is indeed a powerful gift from God and because of that we must learn the proper way to use it. But, what is the proper way? **'WE MUST PROGRAM THE SUBCONSCIOUS MIND SO THAT THE CONSCIOUS MIND CAN DRAW AND PULL POSITIVE SUSTENANCE FROM IT."**

Although the subconscious mind is not programmed to think it does have the capacity to receive any and all ideas or beliefs as a pattern to operate and proceed to bring those same ideas and beliefs into reality. The subconscious mind operates through a system called, **HEREDITARY AND RACE INSTINCT**. Remember when we were children and did things the way our parents thought it should be done? As a result, some of us are still fixated on our childhood rearing mainly because we haven't been fortunate enough to learn the ultimate power of our subconscious mind. But, there are some people who are drawing from this power and truly understand how to use it to their benefit.

I once said to some friends that children are neither bad nor good, it was all about their childhood training. In other words, how the community, the schools, and especially their environment can impacted them and the lasting affect it had. Both children and adults are affected by every thought that enters their minds. When what has been heard is determined to be true, then that information is stored in our subconscious mind. Good or bad, true or false, it's there. Now, the subconscious mind has new information to act on. If we take the time to analyze this carefully, we see that the <u>**SUBCONSCIOUS MIND**</u>

HAS THE POWER TO DETERMINE OUR FATE AND DESTINY.

So, if we are to control our destiny including our health and all the conditions in between, we must quickly learn how to dictate to our minds exactly how we want it to act, or respond. Reminder: Science of the mind teachers normally teach about the super-conscious mind **(THE EGO)** and generally refer to the various stages or levels of inner perfection. But, the truth of the matter is the **SUBCONSCIOUS COVERS ALL ASPECTS OF UNCONSCIOUSNESS.** How do you feel, **"CAN YOU THINK IT?"**

Okay, are you ready to find yourself? Then, let's try digging deep inside of the hidden mind **(THE SUBSCIOUS MIND)** and locate the cells in the brain called **SMART CELLS.** These cells are so smart that they can do several things at one time, they have unlimited capabilities. I would like you to try this – think about the future, now tell your **MIND** that you would also like to think about the present. Remember, in order for this to work you may still need to find that **SILENT**

SPOT that we talked about previously. **THE THOUGHT IT THE CAUSE OF IT ALL**. Therefore, if we store the proper things in our subconscious mind, it will program the thoughts to act correctly. **PROPER THINKING WILL PRODUCE PROPER ACTION**. Ok, now let's start by programming our minds to think positive. And remember, you and I WILL win when our thoughts are the vehicle that we habitually drive.

CHAPTER FIVE
Ideas and Reality

*All the good of the past will only
Guide us if we embrace the idea.
There is nothing new under the Sun.*
- Johnny X Williamson

The Universe produces matter, water, and energy. There is nothing that cannot be invented, discovered, or created. If men and women would only use the powers that are within, they would gain self-mastery because **WE ARE GOD'S SPECIAL CREATION**. Therefore, there are no limits to our potential. Now it's time to call your ideas into being. It will take a second, I said just a second, because that's how long it will take you to say, **BE**!

Once we get in tune with our true selves, we will be able to make sweet music. But I doubt if the best musician in the world could do justice to the person with an instrument that's out of tune. If we are to get the best results in life, then we must get in tune with the infinite mind. Now, if you aren't convinced already that the mind is all powerful, and infinite, you must devote the rest of the day convincing yourself of that fact. When you start believing that there is nothing you cannot achieve, you will begin thinking that you can do the impossible. Remember, **THERE IS NOTHING NEW UNDER THE SUN.** Some scholars and master teachers share the ancient knowing that life evolves because **of IDEAS AND REALITY**. Through thought we are able to create our reality. **THINK BIG AND ALWAYS THINK POSITIVE.**

Is the mind reality? I think that it is. Well, let's start using it as if it is. The Mind is the "real" reality of humans, man, woman and child. This is because everything first originates from an idea. I believe that an idea that is original will find success quicker than an idea that is not. **(A DUPLICATED THOUGHT)**. All ideas have potential power; it's all about how we feed the idea while it's in its 'baby' stages. But, when the idea has been worked on, sometimes the power goes out of the Mind's success window. That is why the original idea should not be tampered with. Please protect your original ideas because they contain dangerous possibility.

I would venture to say that when cave men lived in caves they worked with an original idea. And, the same people who were once cave men, they also are working from an idea, sometimes original, but often times a **DUPLICATED THOUGHT**. Everything is generated from an idea, the same idea that motivates and guides us.

The Mind is a work station capable of working all of the roughness out of the original thought; cleaning it up and smoothing it out so that its power can shine through. Some doctors say that the mind is the best and most powerful aspect of human creation. But, what do you think? I will go a little further and say that the mind is more powerful when its real purpose is revealed. Giving us the insight into how ideas should and must be developed in that work station.

We must remember that initially all ideas are intangible. You can't see the original idea. All we can do is witness the work and faith that comes from it. That's why some ideas never get off the ground. That often occurs when the faith and work factors are not being applied which is required if they are to take 'form.' Unseen forces go to work to make the idea reality. The unseen is called, **CAUSE;** while the seen is called**, EFFECT.** The main reason certain people become successful and winners are not because they are the smartest. It is because they truly understand the power of an idea and because of that they deal with reality in a unique way. And they always are willing to protect a new and original idea. **THE THOUGHT IS THE CAUSE OF IT ALL.**

That which is unseen always acts
before the seen reacts.
I think that all ideas will eventually appear,
Good or bad.

Ideas are the mothers and fathers of all discoveries, both large and small. It is so wonderful that man has the power to control all of the unseen forces that are within him, or her. **(THE IDEA IS INTANGIBLE)**. Father and mother working together will produce the reality, the product or concept. Again, ideas are the producers **(MOTHERS AND FATHERS)** of all religions and philosophies of the world. Ideas have been shared in song, dance, stories, and by the world's divine men of **GOD**. Prophet Jesus once said, "IF YOU HAD FAITH AS BIG AS A MUSTARD SEED YOU COULD MOVE A MOUNTAIN." That is powerful.

In my opinion, man is the highest expression of GOD and in his **<u>MIND LAYS HIDDEN POTENTIAL THAT CAN MAKE HIM GREAT, LIKE UNTO A GOD.</u>** The Universe has a powerful base as does the mind of man. Can man actually make the divine connection with **GOD**? I believe that he can. Not only can he make the connection, he can **WILL** himself to evolve into a God-like creature. **<u>EVERYTHING IS FIRST AN IDEA.</u>**

A great teacher once said that when we commit any act in the realm we call reality; **WE HAVE ALREADY FIRST COMMITTED THE ACT IN THE MENTAL STATE.** **THOUGHT** IS AMAZING. Everything with an origin must first start in the mind before it takes tangible form. If we investigate original man, we see that he was first thought about in the mind of God. After this mighty Supreme Being decided to bring himself forth, he made man in his image. The mind of God is infinite as is the mind of the original man that he created.

Man is capable of any discovery. His ideas stand as the cause of all things, known and unknown. **THAT WHICH IS HIDDEN HATH BEEN MANIFEST OUT OF THINGS WHICH** APPEAR. Do you remember the wonderful story about Aladdin and his Magical Lamp? In the story, all Aladdin had to do was 'rub' this lamp and a GENIE would appear, ready to do whatever his Master wished. It goes on to say that this Genie would make all wishes of the master come true. I believe that the rubbing of the Lamp is a metaphor representing the thought process or the mind of man at work. The Genie represents that hidden power inside of each of us that is awaiting discovery. It all represents the Conscious Mind waiting for instructions from the **SUBCONSCIOUS MIND** as to what direction it should take. I previously said that the mind is only designed to **THINK**, not to act. And when we learn how to properly use our minds, we will be able to sow the seeds in fertile ground and cultivate them into a robust and powerful harvest. No matter what our dreams may be, their fulfillment lies in the Universal Mind of Man. They are ready to come into expression at your or my command.

I trust that you are beginning to think and feel that you have the capability and power to change any and everything about yourself, including your mind and body. By changing your thoughts, you are endowed with the ability to envision new ideas. You have the power to banish all worry and calmly begin changing your present state of mind. Start using your imagination to create a new set of progressive and motivating ideas. Ideas that will push you in the directions of doers and winners; taking out of the range of losers and abusers.

As we get ready for positive change, we must assume the habit of making our minds listen through offering constant **AFFIRMATION TO THE MIND.** We must do this anytime and every time we think it is necessary. <u>**WE MUST CONVINCE OURSELVES THAT WE CAN DO IT.**</u>

Do you remember us talking about the Silent Spot? Ok, let's go there. Whether we are alone or with others, we must constantly tell ourselves that there isn't anything we cannot achieve. There is tremendous power in saying, I AM HEALTHY, I AM STRONG, I AM **POWERFUL, I AM SUCCESSFUL, and I AM BEAUTIFUL.** The primary reason why **AFFIRMATIONS** are important is because they destroy the habits, negative thoughts and ideas that we hold about ourselves that have been accumulated over the years.

Our destiny is fixed to our **SUBCONSCIOUS MIND.** We are not slaves to our circumstances, but the creators of our own destiny. Too often, we blame others for our misfortunes when in fact, we alone are the ones who make our life either productive or poverty stricken and in ruin. **IT'S ALL ABOUT HOW WE THINK**. Sometimes, we even blame GOD for our conditions. But, nevertheless, we are totally responsible for our successes and our failures. **THE THOUGHT IS THE CAUSE OF IT ALL.**

As we grow in our spiritual and mental capabilities, we gain awareness that it is a disadvantage to mix **SICK THOUGHTS** with **HEALTHY THOUGHTS.** Because sick thoughts will attract illness and dis-ease. If you hold any thoughts of failure, please rid them from your thought process so you will not set yourself up to fail. **YOU MUST THINK THAT SICK THOUGHT OUT OF YOUR SUBCONSCIOUS MIND**. This principle states that, LIKE **BEGETS LIKE.** Therefore, **the MORE YOU THINK ABOUT BEING A FAILURE THE MORE LIKELY YOU ARE TO BECOME ONE.**

If the **THOUGHT IS THE CAUSE OF IT ALL** and I know this to be true, then we must diligently concentrate only on what we want. If you feel you aren't impressing a winning desire on your mind, do not dwell on what is not desired – it will make you mentally and/or physically sick and cause you to lack motivation. **ALWAYS INSTRUCT YOUR MIND TO SEE THE GOAL OR DESIRED OUTCOME**. All Universal life principles are one and the same. It is crucial for us to understand that there is but one principle, and that is GOD, the divine principle. In Latin, the word Principle means, **BEGINNING OF FUNDAMENTAL TRUTH**. It is critical that our inner selves see the goal that we are working towards. The Mind is the **THINKER, FEED IT THE PROPER THOUGHTS**.

CHAPTER SIX
The Powerful Emotion Called Fear

The Thought that makes us retreat is fear,
The concept that makes us think inferior is fear,
Low motivation is a product of fear,
And failure is the direct result of fear.
The way that we think is everything.
- Johnny X Williamson

How would you define fear? (1) To be afraid or apprehensive, (2) An emotion that causes a type of action, panic or otherwise, (3) An unpleasant often strong emotion caused by anticipation or acute awareness. These are Mr. Webster's definitions. I personally classify fear this way, "It's a negative and contrary feeling that if not brought under control will eventually abort the progressive movement of the individual." I call this emotion the <u>MIND TRAP</u>. Lastly, fear means,

"FAULTY EDUCATION APPEARING REAL (F.E.A.R.)" Successful people learn how to control and overcome fear.

Man is created in the image of God. What does that really mean? It means that we have the innate power to create. But what will we create, havoc or success? We ultimately have the power to develop a new paradigm of thinking. There is an old saying that theorizes that, **"GOD CREATED ALL OF US, BUT WE MUST MAKE OURSELVES OVER."** A few years **ago, I** can remember dropping to the lowest level of my life's existence. I will not go into the details of my fall, but I will say that I went very low. The point is, we are designers and builders of our own destiny. Bottom line, our lives will not include happiness or joy, unless we can first **IMAGINE THE HAPPINESS AND JOY**. As I was counseling a good friend one day, I still remember telling him that he was setting himself up to fail. He responded, why or how? I said, "For the past 3 hours we have discussed you in a negative image, and the way that you see yourself dooms you to self-destruct." I then told him that he needed to build-up his **MIND SPIRIT,** I was really telling him that he must start seeing himself in a more positive and powerful light. The image is everything,

If success or joy is going to come to us, we better learn how to crystallize the powers that are in us, so that we can defeat the powerful emotion of **FEAR**. Hey, we must tell ourselves that we are no longer afraid. **"I'M NO LONGER AFRAID. WHAT ABOUT YOU?"**

Men and women, plus boys and girls each have their own special type of FEAR. Like I said earlier, sorrow, sickness, and failure spring from fear. Why are we so afraid? It's because we believe in the traditional interpretations of what success is, or should be. Doctors of sociology say that our fears come from false appearances, hereditary environment and race consciousness. But, I think that all these observations are incorrect. I believe that most of us are afraid because we teach ourselves to be AFRAID. These are only negative thoughts that we must know how to think them out of our head and mind. How can we rid ourselves of the negative thoughts? By becoming masters of our information intake system.

We must let our Subconscious Mind and our Conscious Mind come together and form a contract. One that says, 'together, along with a willing participant, US.'

CHAPTER SEVEN
What is Big Faith?

Faith is unseen yet exceedingly powerful,
It is intangible, invisible, and some say mysterious.
But there is nothing under the sun that can move
The impossible like Faith can,
I think that Faith is connected
To the nature of the Most High.
Johnny X Williamson

There was a great man that once said, "If we had faith as big as a mustard seed, we could move the biggest mountain." What kind of faith is that and where can I locate it? That was my question. I think that we must always consider the internal because by doing so we are able to discover the good and the bad that's within us. Good and powerful things are normally buried deep, deep under something either mental garbage or wisdom. Now, if there's mental depth, how can we find it?

As we start shoveling away the unnecessary garbage that makes us feel that we cannot accomplish what we desire or achieve any of our goals or dreams, we may need to take a peek into our hearts and minds **(THE SUBCONSCIOUS MIND)**.

I often tell people that physical beauty is never as powerful as spiritual beauty. I think that I need to qualify my statement. We know that a fashion model needs to be a beauty, that's the physical. But if we extend the beauty, we would have to say that her or his real beauty is internal and based on the attitude and character of the person. Those that discover that hidden beauty early in their career will normally make a bigger impact. They will figure out just how the **MUSTARD SEED PRINCIPLE REALLY WORKS**.

It has been said that dreams are failures, but those who build their futures in their imaginations with faith and purpose will realize their desires. I am not saying that all we got to do is just wish for stuff, and it will drop out of the sky. That's not going to happen. **WE MUST DECIDE WHAT WE WANT AND STICK TO IT.**

HAVING FAITH REQUIRES SOME PATIENCE AND WORK.

I once had the opportunity to meet with a great individual. What was so amazing about him was the faith he had in himself, and the belief that he was able to climb the tallest mountain. He never said, I might, or it may happen, he always said, **"IT IS MINE."** The lesson behind this is, when you claim anything by faith; never undermine that affirmation with negative statements. His poetic theory was, **"IF HE COULD FLOAT LIKE A BUTTERFLY HE WOULD STING LIKE A BEE" (Muhammad Ali).**

There was another former heavy weight champion, George Foreman, who I met when he was no longer the world champion. He was just a preacher. But, he told me that he would become the world champion again. Of course, I laughed, mainly because there was a young 23-year-old gladiator by the name of **IRON MIKE TYSON**. And as far as I could see, there was not a man on the planet earth that would or could de-throne him. So I laughed, but guess what? Mr. George Foreman actually became the **U.S. WORLD CHAMPION** again. **NOW THAT'S BIG FAITH! HE HAD BIG FAITH IN HIMSELF!**

I once had the privilege of meeting a young man by the name of Ernie, the last name isn't important, yet. But when I first met him, he had just been released from a federal prison, and he was telling me that he was going to build **a "BLACK NEWSPAPER FIRM"** in our town, and of course, I kind of laughed at him. The reason why I was laughing was because this was back in the late '70s, and at that time there had never been a black newspaper business in the surrounding area, never. And at that time, I was a very successful business person in the city where he was talking about building his business. I said, **NO WAY**. But, guess what? He not only built a black newspaper company, his firm is now one of the largest newspaper companies in the North Carolina area. **HE HAD BIG FAITH.**

All of these great men never saw themselves as "**MAYBEES**," they only saw themselves as "GONNA MAKE IT HAPPENERS." What is and what was the formula? They understood the concept of having **BIG FAITH**. I'm going to suggest this as a future working goal. When you have determined that you are suffering from little or no **FAITH**, you better do something quickly, if you are to pull yourself out of what I call, the **"POTENTIAL DESTRUCTION TRAP."**

How can we build on our faith? Well, let's ask this question. What would happen if our bodies couldn't get the food that was necessary for a good and strong body? It would probably breakdown, and if not a total breakdown, it would certainly become dysfunctional. We know that we can prevent disease when we supply the body with the proper nutrients that are good and necessary. But, what about our 'No faith' problem?

Like we said previously, faith is intangible. Therefore, it requires an 'intangible solution" which in my vantage point says that **WE MUST FEED OUR FAITH WITH POSITIVE AFFIRMATIONS**, daily. What are we affirming? That we will, we can and we must find success by any means necessary. In other words, failure is not an option for us. We must remember that our **WILL** plays a big part in faith-building, because once our WILL has been fed, we become extremely motivated to bring our goals or plans into the reality state. When the WILL has been properly motivated, your faith will begin drawing from the strength of the WILL, thereby producing a new and powerful desire to achieve. Remember the great men of faith we spoke of, George Foreman, Muhammad Ali, and Ernie, the Ex-con, now newspaper publisher, will then, guess what? All of them had a big amount of personal faith.

What is faith? Faith is something hoped for, but not yet seen. Now the key is to have such big faith in what you hope for that you are positively sure that what you desire is on the way. But, we must remember that **FAITH WITHOUT WORKS IS DEAD**. Don't worry too much, because when your faith has developed to a degree, this force will supply the brain with the required knowledge to bring about that desired goal. And this new founded motivation will project itself from your new discovered FAITH. We can do it, but we must have the desire, the knowledge, the determination, and of course, **<u>BIG FAITH</u>**.

It has been said that we move according to the knowledge that we have. And the element that causes us to expand is our faith. When our faith is small or nonexistent we normally make decisions based on the amount of faith we have. That's why there are people who do big things, and others who see and perform small acts. It's all about how faithful we are in making sure that our ideas and plans come to fruition. Please focus on what faith truly is, **<u>THE SUBSTANCE OF THINGS HOPED FOR, THE EVIDENCE OF THINGS UNSEEN.</u>** Ok, let's think about that for a moment. Without faith we are unprepared. Regardless of our level of education, we still need faith, the more the better. Without faith, we are **'POOR TO DEATH**." Faith is that priceless substance of anything that we desire.

One of the connected reasons why so many people are poor, and are losers is directly linked to how we think, and how big our faith is. The reason that we have not demonstrated more faith is because we do not understand how to use faith, nor do we understand that faith has a divine law connected to it. **FAITH IS BUILT ON THE PRINCIPLE THAT IF YOU USE ME I WILL MOVE IN FRONT OF YOU**. In other words, if we let faith assist us, it will destroy the negative traits of, **FEAR, UNBELIEF, PROCRASTINATION, AND OF POWERLESSNESS**. Faith is the proper food for success and power. Once these enemies of success have been destroyed, we will then have the power and vision to chart out our plans for prosperity. **THINK BIG, THINK SUCCESS, HAVE FAITH**.

If we could, or would embrace the powerful force of FAITH, we would eliminate the idea or notion of placing limits or restrictions on our ability to achieve whatever it is that we are trying to bring into existence. Again, we must start right now believing that every

Thing works in exact accord with the **DIFINITE LAW**. We must build our desires based on our world from within. We were built on hope, courage, and let them be guided by the power of **FAITH**.

I strongly suggest that when those outside negative forces try to knock your ideas down, run from them, get out of their company and view. Because once you let those **SPIRITS DESTROYERS** get in they become just that much powerful. And you must never pay any attention to appearance, because you're and my success will only come from how we think, not how our cloth looks, or how our hair looks. **THE THOUGHT IS THE CAUSE OF IT ALL.**

You must keep in mind that yes faith is powerful, but it must be push with work, faith is deal without work. Your health, happiness, and your success are all in your thought process. You can make your destiny bright or blight. Therefore, if you are not happy with your present condition, you can start changing it right now. How? You have only to visualize them as you would have them in their mature and success stage. And since almost everything is based on **THREE DIMENSIONS,** which means that there is always a beginning, stuff in the middle, and yes there is a conclusion. Now, whatever we do within this operational cycle will depend on how we THINK.

The laws that are setup in the universe will work every time providing we learn how to work with the law that is in effect. I can remember the time when I wanted to start a new Clothing Store, Boy, what a big task. I can remember how I almost killed the idea by the way that I was thinking that it wouldn't work, I did not have all of the funds that were required to start the business, that may have been that I did not have all of the 'know how' that it would take to operate the business. You see sometimes we will kill a good idea by the way we discuss it with our MIND. We must be careful what we feed the mind with. You see, an original idea sometimes does not have the strength to live on its own. You see, ideas are kind of like people, they sometimes need assistance if they are to grow and evolve to a mature stage.

Ideas also have a life cycle, just like humans. When the idea is in the BIRTH STAGE, it will need a lot of parental support, and when the idea starts the growth process, it will need help again. And guess what, it makes no different how good and sound the idea, it will run its course, its absolute cycle, and then it will certainly need further assistance if it is to recreate a new business life cycle. **FAITH IS THAT WHICH IS HOPED FOR, BUT YET TO BE SEEN**, and the bigger the faith, the bigger the potential for success.

CHAPTER EIGHT
Success

The best song hasn't been written yet,
The best house hasn't been built yet,
The tallest mountain hasn't been found yet,
The fastest race hasn't been won yet,
Don't worry or fret,
The chances has just begun,
The race is just beginning.

Johnny X Williamson

We hear all the times about how people talk about success. But, have you ever asked the question. **"WHAT IS SUCCESS?** If we make progress, can we then say that we are successful? There are a lot of standard dictionary meanings for success. I will list a few:

(1) **FAME,**

(2) **POSITION,**

(3) **PRESTIGE,**

(4) PROSPERITY,

(5) STATION IN LIFE,

(6) ACCOMPLISHMENT,

(7) ACHIEVEMENT,

(8) ARRIVAL,

(9) ATTAINMENT,

(10) COMPLETION,

(11) FRUITION,

(12) FULFILLMENT,

(13) REALIZATION,

(14) SATISFACTION,

(15) TRIUMPH,

(16) VICTORY,

(17) WINNING,

(18) GAIN,

(19) BEING OUTSTANDING,

(20) CONQUERING.

I know that you are probably saying that there are a lot of words describing SUCCESS. That is because the concept or opinion of success varies. And because it has different meaning to different people. Let's discuss a few of these meanings before we deal with the writer's interpretation or view. FAME, some people will kill just to be famous, or to just be around a famous person. What is Fame? It is when you are noticed by a mass of people. Most times we will treat famous people as our heroes.

But, is that real and honest success? Prestige, what does it mean? It means to be called Elite or Special, standing out in the eyes of people. It is said that a person who is prestigious normally will demand that other people look up to him or her.

To be prestigious sounds great, doesn't it? And is it really the standard for success? I remember one of my long time friends, Richard T; he told me that he would do any and everything to become a prestigious person. So he joined all of the organizations that were supposed to be prestigious. He would always say that if he was going to make new friends, they would have to be someone great or important. And he continued by saying that his guest list would be made up with people that were going places and doing stuff. Whenever Richard T. would give a cookout, most times some of his family members would be overlooked, by design of course. **I CALLED THIS THE NEED TO SUCCEED FROM GREED AND PRESTIGE.**

Ok, let's take a good look at **SATISFACTION.** What is satisfaction? The standard meaning is **THE QUALITY OR STATE OF BEING SATISFIED**. Being contented. Overall, I kind of like both meanings, because if I'm happy, I should be satisfied, or maybe I should turn it around. Nevertheless, since satisfaction is a mental concept, things that makes some people, will sometimes make others sad or unhappy. **WHAT IS SUCCESS?**

I once took a class called, **"CLIMBING THE LADDER OF HAPPINESS".** The concept was that there would always be a starting place to achieve success. This class, Climbing the Ladder of Happiness, said that when we start any project, large or small, mental or physical, we will need to do the basic and fundamental stuff first. For instance, when we seek personal happiness, there are other needs that we will have to gain first. There are introductory needs, **I CALL THEM, (SECURITY, SAFETY, SOCIAL, FINANCIAL, POLITICAL,** and of course, **SELF ACTUALIZATION**). The need to feel good about one's self is said to be the most difficult to obtain. Probably because maybe we do not truly know what makes us happy. Also, maybe we still don't fully understand the quality of real success. **<u>WHAT IS SUCCESS,</u> AND CAN WE TRULY ACHIEVE IT? AND THE BIGGER QUESTION IS, ARE WE WILLING AND PREPARED TO CLIMB THE LADDER OF SUCCESS?**

Tomorrow is a new day that is full of issues and problems.
In your mind lies either success or failure, or both.
It's all about how we think.
What are you thinking right NOW?

Although we are not discussing Dedication or Discipline, I must make a quick point. If we are to climb the ladder of success, we will have to incorporate the two great principles of progression, which are, **DEDICATION AND DISCIPLINE**. Most times, most people will maintain a positive movement as long as things are going good, but what about when things are going kind of wrong, how do these same people handle the negatives of a situation? Can they continue climbing the ladder of success?

Most times the pain of possible defeat will impede the quality of our performance. It will even make some people stop trying to achieve their goals. I once had a good friend that was extremely good at construction work; he could do the task of five men, and was knowledgeable in a variety of trades, from painting houses, doing cement work, building homes, and many other advanced skills in the construction industry. But after working for other companies for a long time, and because of a few bad years in the construction business, he began to rethink his idea about owning his own construction business. He started second guessing himself to whether or not he had what it took to climb the ladder of success, particularly when things become complex and difficult. I called this the **"JUNCTION OF REALITY",** where the winners and losers separate.

Remember when we said that tomorrow would be full of issues and problems, well, those are natural processes of life, business or otherwise. This is when we must take on an aggressive attitude about climbing the ladder, an attitude that says, **<u>THERE AIN'T ANYTHING OR NO –ONE GOING TO PREVENT US FROM CLIMBING THE LADDER OF SUCCESS.</u>** Because failure isn't an option. Let's go, we got work to do, climb man, or woman, climb.

Lastly, the disease of failure that may be in your mind must be quickly removed. You must bring your thoughts under a new mindset. How should we do it? **WE MUST KILL THE THOUGHTS THAT GRAVITATES TOWARDS FAILURE.** We must cut these negative and unhealthy thoughts off at the root of their origin, which are connected to the thought line, or the chamber of the mind. **THE THOUGHT IS THE CAUSE OF IT ALL.**

CHAPTER NINE
Abundance and Abundance

*Thought by Thought we build our fortune,
And the universe will provide the energy,
Fate is the parallel of Thought,
Select then your destiny and wait,
For good things brings love and bad things,
Hate and oppression....*

Johnny X Williamson

If we are to create abundance, we must try to understand the principles, the law of Abundance. From my research, I've come to the conclusion that Abundance is a natural law. If we would start studying nature, we would quickly see that nature is **LAVISH.** Sometimes Nature is even **"Wasteful and Extravagant;"** for example, every seed that we plant will eventually grow and bring forth many times itself, fifty to a hundred times, and some-times a thousand fold.

Likewise, there is an abundance of Health, Happiness, Love and Prosperity for all of us. And guess what, none of the above qualities are dependent on anyone else; it's all about you and I. We live and die poor or broke mainly because we have not discovered the powerful process of thinking. Almost everything needs some type of support, success is no different. The law of success has partners, and one of the main partners is **THE LAW OF ATTRACTION.** This may sound too good to be true, but, I will say it anyway. Some scholars believe that the Law of Attraction operates unceasingly, and it will bring to you what belongs to you whatever the circumstances. The concept is that what's yours, will find you. In other words, the only one that can stop you is YOU.

I once had a friend who we called, **BROTHER WITH THE MIDAS TOUCH.** It seemed like everything that he would get involved with would turn to gold, or become successful. He was delightful, cheerful, motivating, hopeful and helpful. And yes, he had a million dollar smile. Have you ever had a friend like that, or knew someone who possessed those money making characteristics? Now, compared to this friend, the others who were the opposite, they would always make a bundle of excuses, always complaining, nothing ever seemed to go right for them.

They were bankrupt or sick, or someone had just beaten them out of some of their possessions, it was always a chaos. And there were those that would always find something to criticize, the narrow minded type. I think that if we are a certain type of person(s), then it is possible that the same type of condition or circumstances may gravitate towards you. In other words, failure, loneliness, hard times, poverty, are looking for you.

The Abundance of good and powerful thoughts will attract good and powerful results. I have problems thinking that men and women are good or bad, I must rather think that they are motivated and guided by the way that they think. **THY OWN THOUGHTS SHALL BE THY BURDEN**". Please remember this: **"THINKING ISN'T HEREDITARY, IT'S A LEARNED BEHAVIOR.**

When we embrace the concept of **STRAIGHT REALITY**, we will quickly realize the fact that we express and project absolutely in surroundings and body what we think. And if we can understand that, we would also understand the saying, **"GOD IS GOOD AND JUST."** Reflect on**," THY OWN WORDS WILL BE THY BURDEN."** This should tell us that if we desire good health; we must concentrate on good health. If we desire love, we must learn how to love others; and if we are to have abundance of material things, or anything else, we must think abundance. Ok, I must remind us that thinking in abundance isn't the same as being lavish or extravagant. But, we should also remember that nothing powerful was ever achieved unless we thought a certain way. Some people think negative and small, they normally create on the level of their thinking, while others think large and positive, and they to will project and create based on what and how they think. **<u>THE THOUGHT IS THE CAUSE OF IT ALL.</u>**

    I like using the following example: If you lay a lot of shavings on a barrel, every time someone jars the barrel some of the shavings will fall off; but if you place some magnets under the shavings, you may turn the barrel upside down but the shavings will remain in place. What is the main theory or principle? **IF WE MAKE OURSELVES A MAGNET FOR ANYTHING, OR ANYONE, WE WILL DRAW THEM OR THAT TO OURSELVES.** The Magnet will always pull and draw towards itself. We should always consider avoiding negative magnets. Therefore, we must become positive magnets, thereby attracting positive magnets to us. There are times when we are being pulled by powerful and positive forces embrace them and go with the progressive flow.

Have you ever seen people that work very hard to achieve a goal, and when they get within reach of achieving it, then something bad or critical starts to happen? This unexpected element steps in and will try to destroy the efforts that went into the task of trying to become a success. I have witnessed and have known very talented individuals who would crumble under little pressure. But, I suggest that this is when we must dig deep within ourselves to find the "Will Power" to become more aggressive in obtaining our goals.

Again, I have seen brilliant business persons, who were smart and focused, but did not know how to overcome the difficult factors that relates to business development. These factors would stop them from achieving their original goal. I always would tell them that, **ANYTHING THAT HAVE VALUE WILL ALSO HAVE A DIFFICULTY FACTOR ASSOCIATED TO IT.** You see, as we get closer and closer to obtaining our goals, there is always stuff that comes up that will try to impede the progress and process. I told one of them that he was very close to achieving his goal, and that he should not even think about stopping now, keep going, success is right around the Difficult Factor. On the other side of this issue, there are some people who exert little effort, but they seem to develop winning concepts, and it seems like every-thing comes to them abundantly.

As I talk to business persons, I remind them that **FATE AND LUCK** works for some people, but will work against others. I believe that whatever happens in life is directly connected to the way we think. The cause for every situation, good or bad, may arise from a number of sources. Some experts think that you will be able to judge a man's mental and spiritual capacities by observing his physical condition and the place of his environment.

Some, or maybe I should say, most people think that they have to follow tradition, or be guided by a **"SLAVISH DEVOTION TO THE NORM."** We do what everyone else does; we think and believe with the majority, without even checking or inquiring whether the concept or doctrine is based on soundness, or if what we believe is reality or actual facts. The greatest single barrier to individual progress in based on the above principle, Slavish Devotion to the Norm. I called this the **"INDUCTIVE-v-DEDUCTIVE THEORY."** It works like this; most people use the **DEDUCTIVE THEORY**, which means that they start drawing their conclusions without supporting facts. Now, the **INDUCTIVE THEORY** works in the opposite, it starts from the right side of reasoning and then it gathers all of the facts that are necessary, then they draw their conclusions. The latter method is always the best to use.

The main reason why it is so hard to overcome an established habit is because we often have this tendency to fight any thing that appears to be in opposition to what we think that we know to be true. Some people develop habits of lying regularly because they cannot let go of what they think is real. We will lie, lie, and lie just to protect belief system, for instance, there was a pastor friend of mine's, and he told me that he would certainly go to heaven when he died. I asked him, "Are you sure"? He became so upset and angry; he said the he didn't want to talk about it anymore. He was fixated on what he wanted to be the truth. **THE THOUGHT IS THE CAUSE OF IT ALL.** We battle with any opposition to our traditional beliefs, or perception of the truth. This could be dangerous for those who are attempting to progressively move forward.

I was once asked how we can overcome **ERROR OR MISTAKES.** I thought about the question for a whole day, I then told him that I thought that, "when we figure out how to determine what is factual and truth", we would be able to decrease the number of potential mistakes or errors we makes daily.

But to eliminate all mistakes and errors will be a great and monumental fete. We must gravitate towards our goals and objectives, even under difficult odds. I believe that the MIND has the ability to Detox itself, therefore, we can learn from life's circumstances and mistakes.

When we understand that the mind is the only cell that has the power and ability to deal with Thought. Therefore, the mind can and will create a mental picture or image of whatever it is that we **desire. IF WE ARE TO CREATE AN "ABUNDANTLY FULL AND SUCCESSFUL LIFE, WE MUST LEARN HOW TO THINK A SPECIFIC AND SPECIAL WAY.** Positive Thinking Produces Positive Action.

As I read and studied scripture, I was amazed to how strong and powerful the Bible and Holy Quran were, and are. In the Bible, it stated that, "SEEK YE FIRST THE KINGDOM OF GOD," and then it said, "SEEK YE HIS KINGDOM." I am pretty certain that I was like many others who thought that that scripture was telling us that it was ok to remain in poverty, and to enjoy it. But as I studied it again, this time critically, I eventually got a better understanding of it. My present interpretation is that it meant that if we seek GOD first, all of the other things in life would eventually find their way to our doors. Also, I think that it was trying to let us know how to build and strengthen our Desire and Willpower.

The principle of those scriptures is divinely powerful. They were telling us that if we had the proper desire, there would not be anything that could prevent us from obtaining the ultimate goals that we previously set. Desire is the mental food that will single handedly push us over the top. You see, failure has a top and a bottom component. And when we reach the top of failure, that is where our potential for success resides. If we beat failure, and we certainly can, we will win. And when we figure out just how to over-power failure, we will then be ready to position ourselves to build our kingdom right here on Earth. **BUT WE MUST LET OUR INNER POWERS AND AUTHENIC SELF COME ALIVE.**

The Holy Quran is one of the most read books in the world, it stated that the human-being has unlimited powers. And all that man/woman has to do is to submit him/her self to that higher source of power, or infinite energy. It pointed to the reality that all that man/woman need is already located within them. It also stated that GOD would not assist us until we start helping ourselves .We must motivate the DESIRE that is in us. Man's power is wrapped up in his/her mind and spirit.

So let us read and clear ourselves of the concept that success must come in us, or to us. I think that success must come from us. I stronger recommend that we must quickly get rid of the perception that poverty, distress, disease and sickness only come from physical or biological reasons, NO , I think that the origin of sickness come from the way that we think. I certainly believe that we can get rid of most forms of sickness if we learn how to think them away. **THE THOUGHT IS CERTAINLY THE CAUSE OF ALL MOVEMENT, GOOD OR BAD, LARGE OR SMALL.**

Therefore, if we want and desire a life of fulfillment, filled with Abundance and Abundance, we will have to develop our thoughts, give them instructions, and ride with them. Remember, your mind is the **THINKER, AND YOU ARE THE GUIDE.**

CHAPTER TEN
Man has always had the Power to do for Self

"Man is created in the image of GOD.
God created man in the divine image of himself.
Man is so powerful until he can think.
And then bring whatever he thought of into reality.
What happen to this powerful being that God
Gave all of this original and divine power to? Is he ALIVE?"
                                    Johnny X Williamson

Everything is first a lowly and unproven **IDEA**. But, most ideas die due to the lack of proper feeding. How can and should we feed an Idea? We must feed the Idea with nutritional food of DESIRE .One great writer once said that we can have all of the ideas in the world, but if they are not properly fed, they will ultimately get sick and die. What is an Idea? **<u>AN IDEA IS ONLY A THOUGHT TRYING TO BE BORN.</u>**

Most of us will kill Most original Ideas Most of the time before Most are Born.

Have you ever heard about the Fountain of Youth? Well, a long - long time ago there were some stories about Ponce De Leon, and how he had made himself famous by seeking the Fountain of Youth. Some writers said that it was only a mythical and allegorical joke, and said that the only thing that Ponce De Leon did wrong was to look for youth outside of him-self. I firmly believe that everything that we desire or need is located on the inside of US. What most people, such as Ponce De Leon, didn't understand was that 'Age' is a matter of condition, not years. And that our bodies are constantly being renewed with new energy. Therefore, even if you are 65 years YOUNG, you are still just 11 years old. That is what I'm trying to discuss concerning Thought. Please remember this: Thought does not die because of old age, it will get sick and die from unhealthy thoughts. **<u>MAN HAS ALWAYS HAD THE POWER TO DO FOR SELF.</u>**

What is it that is preventing us from becoming successful or powerful? Is it connected to how we think?

Or maybe it's connected to race, or our life style? I believe that we make ourselves sick, poor, sad, or happy by how we have been programmed to think. But, I also think that we can make ourselves rich,

Powerful and happy; it's all about how soon we get into the process of thinking. Remember**, THINK AND GROW RICH**, rich in what? The **THOUGHT** is the road map for success. Once we get on the THOUGHT ROAD, we must change our thinking patterns, we should never say that we Might, or I will try. In other words, we must say to ourselves, **"I WILL BE SUCCESSFUL."** Ok, that's a good start. Now, since you have spoken the words, that are great to, but, **HAVE YOU TOLD YOURSELF THAT YOU WILL BECOME GREAT OR SUCCESSFUL? OK, SAY IT THEN, "I WILL BE GREAT AND SUCCESSFUL."** It doesn't have to be in that order, but I must warn you that you and I will never become great unless and until we get started. Please remember that if a person can make his/her mind see a thing, he/her can have it.

Now, when I say great, that does not means that I can just go to sleep, and think that everything all good and great, that isn't the reason why I keep saying that **THE THOUGHT IS THE CAUSE OF IT ALL**. I am only trying to get us to see and think you're and my success is on the inside of US. And the only energy that will bring it out is the process of **THOUGHT**. Also, this topic is so crucial to our personal motivation, I just need to make sure that we get it. **THINK BIG AND GROW LARGE.**

That is why I want you to aggressively and constantly tell yourself that you are a winner, and that you will certainly become successful in the near future, or maybe sooner than that. That is why in the earlier chapters, we suggested that you learn how to see yourself as a winner, and to **VISUALIZE SUCCESS IN YOUR INNERSELF, THE SUBSCIOUS MIND**. I realize that I'm asking you to deal with an **ABSTRACT**, that's ok, because we are just in the beginning stage of our development. <u>**MAKE YOURSELF, CONVINCE YOURSELF, AND TRAIN YOURSELF TO BELIEVE IN YOU.**</u>

We normally do what we convince ourselves that we can do. If we send a message to our inner-self, the **SUBCONSCIOUS**, and if that message contains negative vibrations, it will certainly program us to think a specific way, failure, possibly, maybe, and the outcome probably will duplicate how we think and see ourselves. What will happen is that we will place ourselves in the loser bracket at the beginning of the race.

I called this, **PLACING KILLER IMPRESSIONS ON THE BRAIN.** If I could illustrate the point, **WE MUST 'BE' BEFORE WE CAN DO,** or saying it another way, **WE WILL DO EXACTLY WHAT WE TELL OURSELVES WE ARE.** I will take a true life story to make my point. There was a young woman name Lisa, the last name is not important. She was a typical young person that wanted to start her own business, she only had a high school education, but she was very aggressive and smart. She had good natural abilities, plus, she had a charming and powerful personality. She moves a mountain with her big and attractive smile. Those were her positives.

One day I was discussing with her how another one of my friends, Joe, a bookkeeper had become rich and successful in a very short period. She said that she would give anything to learn Joe's secrets, or his method of doing business. She also knew Joe, and she said openly that she knew that she was absolutely smarter than Joe, and that He did not have any more willpower or brains than her. She even stated that she was even a harder worker than Joe. Yet, it appeared to Lisa that everything that Joe touched became a quick success. Why, she screamed. Why? As I looked at her, for the first time since I've known her, there was great despair in her eyes, and I also saw panic and confusion on her face.

I think that the problem with Lisa is a similar problem with a lot of business persons, once they become fearful that they will never get to a greater success level, it will sometimes kill their desire and will-power to achieve their original goal and objectives. What was Lisa afraid of? She was afraid of being placed in the category with the losers. **THE ENERGY OF FEAR IS POWERFUL AND SMART.** I could tell at that very moment that Lisa was letting the same thing that affects most losers affect her, which was the power of negative suggestions influencing her thought process. That is a dangerous position to put yourself in. As I was leaving her, I gave her this advice:

- *Stay focused, and become alive, check yourself from the inside,*

- *Complaining and dreaming is for fools, either you will become a builder,*

- *Or be a tool. Learn to take things as they are, because you are the only real Star…*

If I had to critique my friend Lisa, I probably would say this: You have worked your idea very good, but it appears that your idea has benefited other people more than it has you. You have tried very hard to become a success, but you have returned back where you started, the beginning. Because of your apparent age, you have become seriously frightened of the potential failure, and yes, you are nervous about your future. I call this: **THE PRINCIPLES OF REVERSE EFFORT.** We also will call this the "**FAILURE COMPLEX.**"

What is the solution for this type of problem? Well, the first thing we must do is to destroy all of those bad mental and invisible impressions that are in our Sub Conscious Mind, those that are trying to dictate and control our THOUGHTS, most times in a bad or negative manner. Since we now know exactly where these negatives are coming from, we must speedily drag them out, and **OUT THINK THEM.** Now that Lisa knows exactly where her problem originated from, and where it is now, she can defeat it. I told her that since her main problem started at the beginning of her business, which was the way that she saw herself, she must use herself again, but this time, she must see herself as a Winner.

The theory is, we most of the time create our failure. We often, **sub consciously train ourselves how to fail**. We must now teach ourselves how to win; **THE THOUGHT IS THE CAUSE OF IT ALL.** We must stay focused, check ourselves, stop complaining, take stuff as it is, and think like a builder, not like a tool, and in the end, **WE MUST SEE OURSELVES LIKE AS REAL STARS.**

CHAPTER ELEVEN
Desire Feeds The Will

When things and people are called by their names,
They move quickly, when the sound comes out,
It creates a feeling of Support,
Togetherness and Nearness...
                      Johnny X Williamson

Desire is a powerful emotion; it will guide you through any and all situations. What is DESIRE? It's the food that motivates. If I had to explain success as it relates to movement, I would say that success is when you make movement forward. If I had to explain success in a philosophical way, I guess I would say that success is when the **MIND TAKES CONTROL IN AN ABSOLUTE MANNER, DESTROYIING ALL POSSIBILITIES FOR FAILURE.** If I would explain success in a Political manner, I probably would say, **SUCCESS IS WHEN TWO OPPOSITES MEET,**

THEN HAVE A DISCUSSION, THEN DECIDE WHICH WAY THEY WOULD GO. Desire is a powerful emotion, it will and can move anything.

Whatever decision or choice we will make, one thing is certain, the road to success is through the land of DESIRE. I can vividly see and think back when I had serious problems with finishing stuff that I started, and I would often tell myself all types of good reasons why I could not complete the task. I now realize that my problem was LOW to NO DESIRE. And maybe I wasn't motivated enough to win. And since I did not know how to feed my WILL, it made me to suffer many years, mainly because of how I saw things. The THOUGHT is amazing.

After we reach what I call the stage of Reason and Independent Action, we most times do what we want to do, right or wrong, good or bad. You probably will argue with me on this, and say that conditions and circumstances are just too hard, and your job and duty keeps you from taking a chance at gaining your Desire, but nevertheless, that argument shows a lack of

Motivation and Desire on your part. Also, we must remember that DESIRE is an emotion; you gain it from yourself. Desire isn't a learnt action, it is a **USED ACTION.** I strongly believe that if we would let our 'WILL' be fed with the proper food, which is DESIRE, we would have the power to do all that is necessary to achieve our goals.

Desire will break down anything that stands in its way of success. That is why I teach <u>students/people that when the WILL is properly nurtured, it will search and find keys that will show us</u> how to become successful and free. Free to do what? To plan and to think. I once told a man that had been incarcerated for a very long time; I said to him, **"THERE IS NOTHING THAT CAN KEEP YOU IN PRISON IF YOU TRULY DESIRE TO BE FREE."** And I am telling us today, that there is nothing that can keep us from success but ourselves. We must check our Passion and Desire.

Now, it is very crucial that you remember that your personal power is stored in your Sub Conscious Mind, and yes, it is powerful. It surrounds us like the Sun and the Air. The Mind has Eyes, and they see backward and forward. When we start believing in these facts, we will be ready to think that we can do the impossible, and yes, we will even start to think that there is nothing that we cannot do, even FLY.

Earlier in the book we mentioned that the thought was and is the cause of everything. Therefore, I think that it's appropriate to explain further what I meant. You see, the Mind does its building solely by the power of Thought. The energy of Thought will make us think and act a certain way. For example, if you and I think weak, we will surely act out that weakness. Whatever we form in our minds, it will eventually guide us forward or backward, progressive or regressive.

For instance, when we pray, we form mental images of what we want and think, and if our **FAITH** is strong enough, we will be able to hold our **DESIRE IN OUR THOUGHTS**. This is how we feed the Thought process. I labeled this as the **UNIVERSAL MIND** working in Us. And when we discover our true self, **THIS UNIVERSAL MIND WILL DO THE WORK**

FOR US. This is when you and I will finally believe that there is NO task or challenge we cannot accomplish. I know that this chapter isn't about prayer, but I thought that I should say something concerning how Prayer and the Mind work. I also would like to say that prayer is a guiding force that will open up doors for success to enter. I know that there are some people who have gained enormous success without believing in prayer, that's the exception to the principle. But, I would also say that even if they don't believe in prayer, there is someone in their circle that constantly prays for their success. Prayer connected to Faith will give us the power to think that we can bring our Plans and Desire into manifestation. I'm not saying that GOD will give us all of our Desires; I'm only saying that everything is possible for everyone, even Us. In other words, **"EVERYTHING IS OMNIPRESENT FOR EVERYBODY."** What does this mean? It means that everything that you and I need or want is wrapped up in our **DESIRE**. But, the power that is in us will lay still and dormant if we let it. Or should I say, DESIRE IT. All that we must do is to discover our personal powers, and then begin to use them. We must feed the Desire and Passion.

You are probably saying that you have many Desires, and you certainly would like to be rich, happy and successful, but most of us have habits of doubting ourselves. WRONG, WRONG, WRONG. Many of us will quickly say that we don't truly believe in this mind stuff, and that it sounds too much like Psychology. But there are some who will give a new idea or concept a try. For the sake of success, **LET US GIVE THIS A TRY.**

I think that many of us have these 'minor desires', and most times we can't see, or believe that we can actually achieve many of them or any of them. I have labeled this as, **BEING TRAPPED IN** lots of stuff, and most times they don't do all that is available or possible to secure their wish or desire. Maybe it is because they don't believe in it, or in their self. Or, maybe it is because they haven't discovered that the" **WILL MUST BE FED BY DESIRE IF WE ARE TO ACHIEVE THE GOAL".** Once we decide on exactly what it is that we want and desire, we must speedily rebuild our Self-

Esteem and Motivation so that they will unite with our Desire. If we do this, our Desire will open the doors of success and happiness for us, and remember that true Desire gives us new energy, which is directly connected to the **THOUGHT PROCESS.**

If there is such a thing as a magic secret of Attainment, I would have to say that it is, **"ELIMINATE THE MULTIPLE DESIRES!"** Fix one goal at a time, concentrate on just one desire. If I could use a mountain to illustrate my point, I would say it like this, 'when you are climbing a mountain, you would not start on one path today, and another path tomorrow. That means that you probably would never reach the top of the mountain. You must make yourself, and then train yourself to entertain ONE DESIRE at a time. Because when these minor desire grow into real desires, that is when you are approaching the realm of SUCCESS. Success is right around the corner, keep going, and keep thinking. **THE IDEA IS ONLY A THOUGHT, AND THE THOUGHT IS THE CAUSE OF IT ALL.**

The nice home, beautiful family, children and wife, whatever the desire, you must place it in your mind, fixate it there, and then you must claim it, declare it, and you must believe and understand that whatever you desire, it's yours. But please remember, you must station your desire in your mind firmly. **FROM THE MOMENT YOU DESIRE ANYTHING, IT BECOMES YOURS TO HAVE.** Please lock this new desire into your heart, so that the **LAW OF GROWTH CAN TAKE ROOTS.**

DESIRE is like a corn seed, a potato seed; they all have the same nature as it relates to growth. In other words, all of them must be Planted. If we plant seeds in the garden, but after a little while, we dig them up to see if they have sprouted, and then throw them away, and plant new seeds, they will never take root, and of-course they will not produce the product or results. **THE THOUGHT MUST BE PLANTED IN THE MIND FIRMLY.**

There are laws that govern the growth process, those laws apply to almost everything that grows or evolves.

Whether it is mental or physical, there is a law(s) in affect. Now, after planting our seeds, we must feed them with **THOUGHT, EXPECTATION, CONFIDENCE AND DESIRE. "DESIRE IS THE FATHER OF MOTIVATION."**

Remember when we discussed the power of the Sub Conscious Mind, and how we said that it works in regards to achieving the goals, well, if you can establish in your mind that something is yours, I believe that your Sub Conscious and Conscious Mind working together will show you how to obtain it. There isn't anything that we cannot do when our minds are working for us, and with us. It is said that most people start out with a single goal, and then add on. Therefore, figure out what is your goal and go for it. There is No One or Anything that will stop you from **YOUR** success, but you and your Thoughts. One Idea, One Thought at a time is the answer, unless you have the ability to departmentalize Multiple Thoughts.

Imagine things as you want them, build on new ideas, stay with the **SINGLE DESIRE AND GOAL,** and please stop thinking that some people are born to be poor, and others rich. Destroy that unhealthy thought right now, because it will destroy your Desire. You and I can have anything that we want and desire if only we would convince our MINDS TO ASK FOR IT. Desire is powerful; Desire is the proper food to feed the '**Will**'. Some others say that our bodies and minds reflect who inherently we are.

Some times we list our habits in order of importance. We normally say that **DRINKING, GAMBLING, USING DRUGS,** these were the negative/bad ones. Now the good ones, **ALWAYS BEING ON TIME, TELLING THE TRUTH, FAITHFUL CHURCH GOER, AND CHECKING ON THE OLDER CITIZENS, AND CHECKING ON THE COMMUNITY 'SOUP KICHEN'.** By thinking this way, we probably will overlook the habits that maybe more harmful or better for us. Some other habits that may harm us are, **FEAR, WORRYING, ANGER, JEALOUSY,** and of course, the emotion of **ENVY.** I call these the mother and father of negativity. These are very serious and dangerous habits, therefore, we must find ways to destroy or control them.

I know that we can't always prevent things from happening, good or bad, but, I know that we can certainly create or develop the HABIT of self control, and what happens does matter, but your and my reaction is what really counts. Habits will cause us to win, or to lose. WE must remember that discipline of control is everything. Looking at it another way, stuff that causes some people to commit suicide, will motivate others to achieve their goal, small or large.

I am determine to destroy my bad habits, and will use discipline and control of my good habits. I will train myself to smile in the face of defeat. Not that I'm planning to fail often. My mishaps and misfortunes will be my propeller to success in the future. **I WILL ULTIMATELY WIN.** As close this chapter, I want to suggest to us that we take stock of our happiness. We must destroy any and all habits of **THOUGHT AND ACTION** that does not enhance or contribute to our happiness. We must isolate and uproot those unhealthy habits right now. Sure we may fall from grace sometimes, but remember that we must stay in the game of **THOUGHT.** Whatever the real cause of any habit, I think that we can overcome all of those nasty and ugly negative habits, and we will learn how to replace them with positive ones. I believe that if we are to acquire the freedom from wants and needs, we must gain a new attitude. This new attitude will bring a new set of bright ideas, and we will find ourselves on a new plane with everything changed, including **OUR HABITS. <u>(THE THOUGHT IS THE CAUSE OF IT ALL)</u>.**

CHAPTER TWELVE
THE RUTS OF LIFE

"Whatever the issue, whether It's Mental, Physical, Religious, Economical, Financial, Spiritual, Social, Simple or Complex, most times they are difficult to Get out of. Why? Because all of the above represents A difficult factor that must be defeated……..The Mind is the First and last option that must be used when getting out of the Ruts of Life"

Johnny X Williamson

There are many- many reasons that cause people to fail in life. Some are small reasons, and others are large and complex. . What are we talking about when we use the term **RUT**, What is the meaning? The term Rut has literal and allegorical meanings. For instance, the literal meaning is that when we are in a Rut, we are in a ditch or hold like condition. The allegorical meaning implies that we may have some mental and emotional issues that we can't overcome. Either way, these are serious Ruts that we need to figure out how to defeat of control them. The amazing thing about Ruts are they may be created by you/us, or they can be created by other people associated with us. Getting in and out of Ruts will take work. One thing to remember, getting into a Rut is always easier that getting out of one,

I was once told by a well known doctor that when and if we get into Rut, we better know how to quickly get out of it. He said, "Sometime if we don't get out quickly, we may end up in that Rut for 20/30 years, and he said that some people will never get out." One great leader once said that there are some people who know how to take advantage of being place in a ditch like condition. He illustrated his example of the Donkey falling in a ditch, and when people would come by they would through stones in the ditch on top of him, the Donkey. This great leader said that the Donkey used the stones to climb out of the ditch. Therefore, the lesson that we can draw from this is that we can use downfalls as stepping stones. That was the physical Rut, what about the physical and emotional Ruts?

Like was mentioned above, the physical ruts will require the same emotion to solve the problem as does the mental ruts. Why? Because both demands and requires that greater Thought be applied to the issue. There will have to be a desire to get out of the ditch; likewise, there must be a mental and emotional desire to climb up into a new way of thinking about the issues that places us in bad situations, **The Rut.**

Let's discuss some of other the ruts that will cause us to fail. What about the Rut called **LASINESS?** Laziness is so critical that if we don't defeat it, it will certainly destroy our chances of ever finding success or progress. **LASINESS** will throw us over board and will eventually cause us to drown from **INACTIVITY**. In other words, laziness is like being on a plane that is literally going to crash. Laziness must be defeated. What about the Rut called Fear? What is fear? Fear is the mother of Failure. The meaning of fear is: **F.E.A.R**, False Education Appearing Real. Therefore, the facts and concepts that guide us or motivates us must be based on reality. The only real and lasting way to defeat fear is to defeat it with **TRUTH**. When we use truth to guide us in making decisions, Falsehood will run-a-way. **TRUTH AND FALSEHOOD** will not and can not occupy the same space at the same time. Where does Fear come from? I think that Fear comes from a section in the Brain that is easily manipulated by negative vibrations that flows in and out of the Brain.

One of the basic elements of Fear is **ANXIETY**. Being unsure or uncertain of the future. In other words, you can think yourself into Fear. Once you become afraid, all of your decisions will reflect the degree of your fear. Please remember this important analogy, which is, Fear is nothing but an emotion, therefore, if we can bring our emotions under control of our Power Base, which is THOUGHT, we will be able to overcome any and every thought that runs through our mind.

What about the Rut of Bad Company? Some doctors teach that you are judge by the company that you keep. Which if true, we better watch out for bad company. For instance, if you hang around 9 broke individuals, the Law of Average states that you will probably be the 10th broke individual. I think that being in a state of poverty, being homeless, being alone, and being broke is a direct factor and element of being fearful. What are we afraid of; most of us are afraid of ourselves. Why, because our present self has been program to fail. And guess what, all of these emotions are cause by the way that we think.

What about the Rut of Procrastination? This is probably one of the most serious Ruts that we can be in, why? Because procrastination has tendencies to make us put stuff off, to wait on other people to act, to become slow at making important decisions. Procrastination is the biggest enemy to success that we will ever have. Don't you think that it's time for us to get out of the Ruts that we are in? I do.

Lastly, please remember that these ruts are Manufactured by US, and are guided and motivated by internal factors, but there also are many external factors that will create these Ruts for us. Either way, they can be brought under our control, how? We must create doors and windows in our Mind that can only be open from the inside. Why? Because we must be able to determine what we want in, and what we want to go out. Our Thoughts are the only thing that will make us or break us. Lest get out of these Ruts and get on the road to "Our" success. It all about how we think**. "THE THOUGHT IS THE CAUSE OF IT ALL"**. President Barack Obama once said that **"YES WE CAN".** This was only a thought when he first said it, but because his vision was so powerful when it came to negative influences, He prevailed. **"YES WE CAN".**

CHAPTER THIRTEEN
Finding Your True Self

You cannot stay on the outside
Of yourself looking for the true essence of yourself.
You look from within the inner chambers of your SPIRIT.....
                                            Johnny X Williamson

Sometimes it will take a life time for man or woman to truly discover their true self. I use to think that other people were given greater opportunities than I. Yes, that was a bad habit. But I recently discovered that those that I thought were born with better and greater opportunities, I now know that they were the ones that worked hard at creating their own opportunities, most times faster than others.

My point here is that your **TRUE SELF** is your spirit. And that spirit is the only resource that we have that is totally and forever complete. This spirit that I'm talking about will remove all limitations that our mind sometimes places on us, or maybe I should say, IN US. I'm talking about those limits that will tell us that we can't continue, and we must stop before we achieve our goal. We must overcome those difficult factors that tell us to quit. Although we have these desires to do stuff, if we aren't careful, we will trap ourselves into the FAILURE TRAP. We must always remind ourselves that whenever we take on a task that seems to be impossible, or extremely difficult, we must tell ourselves that we got to take off the gloves of Limitations, and put on the gloves of everlasting power. Even when we lack the great educational achievements, or the environmental training that is sometimes necessary to make advancement, we can always call on the most powerful force in the universe, which is **FAITH.**

Another powerful force that will assist us in finding our true self is **AFFIRMATION.** How? If we constantly tell ourselves that we are winners over and over again, our inner spirits will begin to assist us with finding our true spirit faster. **OUR SPIRITS ARE**

WAITING ON US TO CATCH UP WITH OUR DESIRE.

Affirmation is a wonderful way to establish your knowledge of your real self. Even when you are healthy, smart, beautiful, young, old, happy or sad, rich or poor, you must repeatedly tell your conscious mind that you are someone that is important, and **SOMEONE WHO WILL NOT ACCEPT FAILURE AS AN OPTION.**

Now, when you make these **AFFIRMATIONS**, if they are to work and have power, you must first become a believer in what you are telling yourself. In other words, your **MIND** will work with you and for you, but please don't send it the wrong message or mixed signals. This method will assure you that your DESIRES will in a positive manner.

I am now at a point in my personal development, that when I tell myself over and over that the goal is achievable, and I intend to make it happen, right then and there, nothing or no one will keep me away from the objective and goal. Nothing under the Sun, but **GOD** will be able to stop me. Therefore, I know that I will achieve the goal, because I know that **GOD** will not stop 'good-progress'. Remember, you must be certain that you will carry out your desired goal.

Ok, let US, you and I start with a small but important **AFFIRMATION**. Are you ready for success? First say this, **"I WILL ACHIEVE THE GOAL"**. If you will say this to yourself several times, and make yourself believe it, then success will become your reality. Make sure that your intentions are noble and good. We would hate to affirm the negative desires or wants.

There are three very important ladies in my life Doris, Sadie and Sabrina. Doris is my baby sister; she is honest, hard working, and always deals with high integrity. Sadie, she is my aunt, but we were raised up as twins, she is a few months older than me. There isn't anything she will not do for me, I adore her. Now, Sabrina, she is my oldest child. She has some of the same qualities as the other two women in my life, and she also has a keen insight on business. She presently is the CEO of a not-for-profit organization called the **I CARE SUPPORT GROUP**. All of these ladies have a certain type of influence on how I make decisions. My sister, Doris is academically inclined; she received her Business Administration several years ago. I'm impressed with her because of how she sets goals and then go out and make it happen. Sadie, she's the smart one in the group, but, she never did go to college, but she has always been excellent in how she use her money. Lastly, Sabrina, she has great ideas, hard worker, dedicated, and yes she's determine to become successful. Her challenge is to develop a mindset that she must develop one project at a time, because one will have to be trained extensively in how to direct the mind in dealing with multiple thoughts at the same time. All of these ladies made themselves strong by learning how to affirm early in their life.

I CALL THIS THE POSITIVE AFFIRMATION FACTOR. The point is, I believe that it is great to have strong women behind or in front of you, when you are trying to achieve your goal.

CHAPTER FOURTEEN
Tuning In To You

*"Tune in to God and live, tune in to yourself and grow,
And if you analyze yourself passionately,
You will find the hidden keys to Success"....*
　　　　　　　　　　　　　　Johnny X Williamson

Although we have learned to ignore appearances, yet it is still very critically important to guard your **THOUGHTS** diligently. Also, make sure that you keep your mind focused on the goal. Keep your mind on a hopeful and happy plane. Always make sure that you instruct your mind to the fact that it must always be ready to move forward. And if there is any type of retreat, it's only tactical.

It may be that the gift of tuning in may be the greatest gift that humans received from God. Why?

Because, when we are able to actually tune in, we will gain the power and the potential to master our own destiny. Also, we are able to tune in; we will be able to place our conscious mind **IN TUNE WITH EACH OTHER.**

Some people will say that it is impossible to tune in with another human, and even may say that it is nonsense. Nevertheless, I strongly believe that not only can we tune in with our mind, we can actually tune in with the minds others. But, self tuning in is necessary if we are to be able to tune in with others. Maybe I should say, KEYING IN. The mind of man is like the universe, capable of solving any and all task, mental or physical.

Therefore, you should be able to grasp the reality that if your thoughts are blue and discouraging, your attitude will certainly be blue and discouraging also. What is the principle, well, if you think dreary and negative thoughts; you will project the same image, physically and mentally. Now we must warn you, that if our thoughts are blue and negative, we will have thoughts of poverty, disease, and distress. On the other hand, if your thoughts are positive and clear, hopeful and happy, you will receive the best positive energy from a positive mind. And when this happens, you and I will be ready to **TUNE IN, OR KEYING IN. One of the Greatest leaders in the world, The Hon. Minister Louis Farrakhan, stated that at one time "Man was able to Tune In with each other."**

Academic and Eternal knowledge is great, but I would always say that the best knowledge is to **KNOW THY SELF**. Most times teachers are critical of our development, but when the teacher **is NO-LONGER** present, this is when we must be able to go deep within ourselves, analyze, and pull out from what is stored in us.

The hardest work, or task that we have is to learn how to **DEPEND OWN OURSELVES**. This isn't easy, mainly because for the most of our lives we have been trained to let someone else lead or guide us. That probably was fine when we was children, but since we are matured adults, I think that we should get in the habit of thinking and doing for ourselves. What do you think?

Sometimes we will have to work with others, but depending totally on them is a big **SIN.**

I think that this is one of the problems that our youth are facing today; they seem to depend on **MOM and DAD** to the extreme. It is very important that we teach our youth to develop a certain level of self dependency. When we go to college we immediately began to depend on our future **BOSS** to make a way for us. Again, that was good when we was children, but we are grownups now. I am not saying that we should not seek work from others, But, I am suggesting that that choice be secondary. We should never depend on others to create what we are capable of creating.

Ok, after you have tuned in with yourself, and after you have learned and decided to do for self, what are the real benefits? The number one benefit is that when you know that you must equally depend on YOU. This feeling and attitude will guide and push you to achieve whatever it is you are attempting to obtain. Secondly, once you get started **KEYING IN, AND DOING FOR YOURSELF,** all of those inferior thoughts will leave you, and they will find a weaker mind to occupy. **DEPEND ON YOURSELF, TUNE IN NOW.**

CHAPTER FIFTEEN
The Principle of Silence

*Sometimes when we speak, our words project Wisdom.
Sometimes we can project the same energy
By staying completely silent or still...*
                                        Johnny X Williamson

A person once said to me that to be silent means to be in agreement with. I totally disagreed with his perception and interpretation. I would also like to point out that when we are silent, under specific circumstances, silent does talk. I think that **SILENCE MAY BE THE FORCE THAT UNLOCKS THE MIND AT TIMES.**

When we are searching for success, sometimes it isn't necessary to discuss all of our plans and affairs with other people. Staying silent definitely works. Now, there is a time and place for everything. For instance, you and I are about the discuss our business plan, but there are strangers near us, is this the best time, of-course not. **SILENCE IS THE KEY.**

Unless it is necessary to discuss your desires and plan for a business venture, please don't talk about what you wish or plan to do. Good Ideas are stolen every day. Always dedicate yourself to serious thought about your desires and business objectives. And remember, **LET YOU BECOME YOUR ADVISOR AND COUNSEL SOMETIMES.**

I know that there's a certain degree of personal satisfaction when we tell friends and associates about our future goals and plans, but most times this is a waste of time and energy. **ITS NICE HEARING OURSELVES, ISN'T IT?**

Normally, most of the people that constantly brag about all the stuff that he/she will do, they never seems to get it done. Most times they end up doing the opposite, nothing. Please keep silent about all of your business matters. When you have a good idea, stick it up in your mind, and guess what, that idea will give added personal power. Why and How? "**BECAUSE SECRETS STIMULATE AND INTENSIFY YOUR THOUGHT PROCESS.**"

Also, there is another powerful benefit for staying silent sometime, which is, **IF YOU ARE NOT TALKING, THAT MEANS THAT MAYBE YOU ARE BUSY LISTENING.**

CHAPTER SIXTEEN
The Invisible Design (The Pattern)

We as humans have yet to discover our true potential.
Our true force is buried in a sea of disbelief and fear.
Our real greatness is directly connected to the reality of GOD...
Johnny X Williamson

If we are to maintain and survive on Earth, we as humans will always need life sustaining elements, which are oil, water, and certainly, food. For instance, in the vegetable kingdom, there are thousands of different types of trees and flowers, and each draws the stuff that is necessary to sustain its life. But guess what, those trees and flowers colors and forms are decided by Nature's secret pattern. I call this, **THE INVISIBLE FORCE.**

In the Animal kingdom we can take some kittens or baby puppies, and feed them the exact same food, keep them precisely in the same space, and care for them the same way, but in the end, both of them will develop their color, form, and characteristics from its own breed, because, regardless of the material condition, the unseen pattern, the invisible pattern, will be apparent in each breed.

What about man and woman? As it relates to man and woman, of course they are unique in every sense of the word. Like we have previously said, we can give babies the same food, each representing a different type, and the consciousness of each type will manifest the pattern for its personal growth, color, and unique characteristics. The mold and pattern of humans exist on the unseen side of life, and will and must express inexact accord with its own consciousness. **THAT IS THE DIVINE LAW OF THE UNSEEN NATURE.**

I ALWAYS TELL STUDENTS THAT WINNERS ARE NOT BORN, THEY ARE INFACT 'MADE'. We make decisions by our own consciousness. And yes, Man has the ability to set his own course of action, or inaction. All of us have the creative power to build ourselves individually by working on the stuff that keeps us down. Man can create his own unseen pattern. I know that I have mentioned this unseen pattern several times during this chapter, the reason is because I want us to get the essence and meaning of **"HIDDEN POWER, WHICH IS CONNECTED TO THE "UNSEEN PATTERN".**

This hidden power will bring us up to any level. Now, those of us who have discovered this HIDDEN POWER, they will normally become winners in a aggressive style, I have never truly done any research on what causes some to win and other to lose, but I would bet that it has something to do with this Hidden Power. This Unseen Pattern is the World of **"CAUSE and AFFECT"**

So, if you and I desire to find true power, we must start by developing our true potential. No Man/Woman has yet measured their true force. Find your true potential, and you will also locate **your HIDDEN PATTERN AND YOUR HIDDEN POWER.**

CHAPTER SEVENTEEN
Caution and Reflection of Reality

There is nothing under the Sun that
Does not belong to you and me,
Nothing. Everything on our planet is a gift from God....
                                    Johnny X Williamson

Your and My Mind in their present state of development has the potential to control the universe. Our present Sub-Conscious Mind determines precisely what we are right now. What does this mean? It means that if we are to figure out how to pull positive energy from our Sub-Conscious Mind, we will place ourselves in a powerful position, one that will enable us to change any condition over night. But, please don't jump to conclusion that you can read the truth from a book and then go right out and begin manifesting a completely new set of conditions.

The mighty oak tree didn't become mighty in the beginning, it took many years. The Acorn that started the process was a tiny little seed, but after the Law of Growth get involved, it will propel this little seed into a mighty big oak tree. The same process applies to little ideas, they may start small, but if we feed them with the proper fertilizer, that small idea will certainly grow into a mighty big success.

There is one unique and different ingredient that is found in Man that isn't found in the Tree, It's called the **Ability To Reason.** Also, the spirit that guides the human is not subjective to time as is the tree. **MAN IS THE ULTIMATE REALITY…..**

People that place limits upon themselves will normally place blinders on their minds. Thereby, making it almost certain that they will not achieve their goals. It is almost impossible for that type of Thinker to Succeed. Some people can never imagine themselves making a Million Dollar, but those same persons can see themselves spending a Million Dollars. How can we change this defeating concept? **THE THOUGHT IS THE CAUSE OF IT ALL.**

The first thing that we must do is to see ourselves as WINNERS. Then we must take away the Props and Cuffs off of limitations. If we can change the way that we perceive and think, and we certainly can, we will ultimately be able to direct and change our overall condition. To keep some equilibrium, we must 'overhaul our **CONSCIOUSNESS.**

After we develop a new Consciousness, new ideas will come, which in turn will make new and bigger demands on our Minds to guide us to meet and achieve our goals. These demands will be met in perfect accord with the UNSEEN PATTERN, or the mental picture held by us. Bottom line, if we are to succeed, we will have to THINK. Caution and Reflection of reality is a great path for change.

CHAPTER EIGHTEEN
The Time Factor

When you are on time, it is a plus,
If you are late, progress may stop,
Procrastination is the enemy of Success,
Time is the greatest factor in the
Scope of progressive evolution,
Time will make a big difference in
Winning or Losing…..

Johnny X Williamson

Time is certainly a big factor in the process of action. But, time is not a prime factor in the building of our Consciousness. Some people are able to get results quickly, while others may take months or years before they will see any results. Some people are able to grasp a complicated set of designs in two hours or less, but others may take longer, and still will-not fully understand it.

You may have the ability to learn more in ten minutes, because of your intense concentration, than you could in months of ordinary thinking habits. Someone once said, "**THERE IS A TIME AND PLACE FOR EVERYTHING**". Therefore, the next question is: "**THE TIME AND WHAT MUST BE DONE.**" (**By: Minister Louis Farrakhan**). I think that both of these sayings sum up my point and premise concerning **TIME**. Time waits on No One.

Our success and progress depends on our ability to 'eject' old ideas and the traditional belief system. We normally move according to our perceptions and opinion. There is one good thing about having a set of opinions, or a belief that your idea or opinion must be right at all times. We must remember that each generation will bring forth new and scientific facts that will set aside what we think are true. **TIME IS A GREAT VEHICLE FOR MOTIVATION.**

There will be no progress without change. Therefore, we must always keep an open and willing attitude for learning. Some people never get past the beginning,

WHY? Because they will declare everything false because they just don't understand the design or concept. I suggest and recommend that all of us need to dig in deep and find out what **TIME** is. What is Time? Time is defined as the measured or measurable period during which an **ACTION, PROCESS, OR CONDITION EXISTS OR CONTINUES.** The point or period when something occurs. Time will always have a beginning and ending. **(The stuff that occurs in the middle is critical).** Now is the time for us to take a serious and friendly interest in everything that relates to us.

The Good Book said that there is a time to cry, a time to die, a time to play, a time to be serious; in other words, there is a time and place for everything. If we are not on time, we are probably wasting time. I am convinced that it is the right time for all sincere men and women of the world to work together for change. With the expectation of making the world better. We must decide right now**, (TIME)** that we are willing to die if need be, in order for us to create a better and safer world.

We can no longer put off this important action. One great person once said: **"IF NOT NOW, THEN WHEN?"** There are times when we as humans need to be separated**. NOT NOW**. It is time for complete unity. The world is so messed up, we should not think that one group of citizens will **be** able to solve all of the serious problems that linger over our country**. WE NEED A MULTITUDE OF POSITIVE THINKERS AND DOERS**. It's about time for US to check out how America operates. Why? Because this present system is in serious chaos. Although we are the richest country on the planet, by far, we are still plagued with issues that seem unsolvable. We have a lot of bright individuals, but we still find ourselves bogged down in racism, poverty, inferiority, superiority, and other ISMS that are destroying us as we write. What's the solution? We need thinking men and women who are emphatically interested in making the world a better place for all of us to live, work, and to strive for our personal success.

By now, I know that we all should be thinking of methods and ways to evolve in the direction of prosperity and happiness, I am**. THOUGHT** is one of the fastest energies that travel. Thought moves faster than the speed of light. faster even than sound. It is said that God created the world in 6 days that is extremely fast. How fast does **TIME** travel? It was also stated that God created the World from the process of THINKING. **"THE THOUGHT IS THE CAUSE OF IT ALL."**

As we come near our conclusion, I think that it is appropriate and nice if we would leave the readers with some recommendations and suggestions on how to go forth towards success. Also, we are challenging the readers to do all that is possible to become successful in whatever goals that are set by them. I would like to suggest to you a Master Menu for success. Also, please keep in mind the purpose of this book, which is to let us know how powerful **THOUGHT** is. If the below recipe is consumed, I think that we would be able to achieve success at a greater and faster rate.

CHAPTER NINETEEN
Dr. Johnny X
Menu For Success

Opinion Number One: "Personal Honor"

One of the greatest forces in Man is his HONOR. Without honor man is weak, and he will certainly and eventually destroy himself. An honorable person will always try to be true to himself, and will do the same towards others. Honor is when you see other people in the same light as you see yourself. I believe that if and when a person achieves greatness, the principle of HONOR was guiding him or her. Honorable individuals work extremely hard at building and maintaining a solid reputation. Bottom line: I BELIEVE THAT HONOR IS

PROBABLY THE GREATEST ATTRIBUTE THAT MAN/WOMAN POSSESSES. (Stay Honorable).

Now, we must keep in mind that all people will not embrace the concept or idea of honor; nevertheless, you and I know that this is the proper course of action that is positive and beneficial. Also, we know that those who are not honorable, they are probably not positive thinkers either, STAY HONORABLE.

Opinion Number Two: "Develop Your Inner Strength"

There are powerful forces in us that will automatically push us, or pull us in positive or negative directions. As we have mentioned previously, it will take our inner strength being tapped into if we are to overcome the pitfalls of failure. We must discover that unique power that is internally asleep, but is desperately waiting for us to wake it up. We must try harder than ever before to wake up our INNER MOTIVATION, RIGHT NOW! Some people call this force the DESIRE OF NEED. I call it the "SPIRIT AGENT". If we develop the inner strength, the SPIRIT AGENT will guide us to success.

Opinion Number Three: "Always Be Respectful To Self and Others"

There are certain elements in a person's behavior that is more important than others. One of these elements is RESPECT. Respect to me is probably the same with most people, so the question then becomes, how do we view RESPECT? Respect is when a person thinks as highly of others as he does himself. For example, when a respectful person makes any type of deal, he/she will consider the other person(s) that is involved in the transaction or situation. Because of the power that comes from respect, it makes some people think that it's a 'Sin' to disrespect others, or to be disrespected by someone. Some even think that those persons that disrespect others will be cursed by God, I don't go that far, but I would like to say that without respect, some of us would never get to the top.

Opinion Number Four: "Have The Courage To Try"

When ever life gets hard of difficult, appearing as if it's a sure defeat. I am strongly suggesting that this is when we must frantically start digging deep down within ourselves to find the ability to continue, this is absolutely essential if we are to locate our COURAGE SPRING. When and if all odds are against you, courage is one of the forces that will propel you to the next level. Courage is when you make up your mind and spirit that you will not stop until the goal has been completed.

Some people are so filled with Courage, until they will trick themselves, their minds that the desired goal has already been achieved, and that they are now working only to preserve the success. There is one thing that we all should remember, which is, when defeat seems apparent, and it looks like the possibility of winning is out of the question, remember, that you may be in striking zone of success, and yes, it may be right around the corner. DISCOVER YOUR COURAGE AND YOU WILL PLACE YOURSELF IN THE GAME OF POTENTIALITY.

Now, as we spoke earlier, everything has an opposite. What is the opposite of Courage? It is Fear. What is Fear? Fear is: FAULTY EDUCATION APPEARING REAL.

Opinion Number Five: "You Must Defeat the Opposites"

Facts state that everything has a negative and a positive. Facts also state that there is a cause and effect for every action. Therefore, if we are to place ourselves in the winner's circle, we will have to learn how to understand these facts, because truth –v- false are opposites, and like we have previously stated, Success –v- Failure are the apex of the opposites.

My suggestion is, if we are to deal with the opposites, or the negatives and positives, we must figure out how to deal with the reality of Failure. <u>HOW CAN WE DEFEAT FAILURE</u>? We must make sure that our successes defeat our failures. Guess what? In life there will always be both. But if we can preponderate our success rate, our failures will come under our control. The way that this work is like this: Since success has a starting point, most times in the beginning, failure also has a starting point, most time in the beginning. We must be determined to overcome the failure at the beginning, why? Because this is when you and I will tell ourselves that we will Win or Lose. Since failure has this starting point, we must be determined to overcome the failure at the beginning, or whenever our thoughts start programming us to fail. When these secondary thoughts, what I call the "Failing Thoughts," get to the top of our original Idea, the original thoughts, we gotta be ready to climb right over them. REMEMBER THE LADDER OF SUCCESS? We must use the Ladder.

Please remember that all of the opposites are working against each-other. We call this, "POSITIVE AND NEGATIVES ENGAGED IN SUBDUCTION". All of these opposites are working side by side, pulling, pushing and certainly trying to defeat the other opposites.

Lastly, keep in mind that we will never win at any contest, unless we get to the top of the failing opposites. I will say this: Dedication and Mental Discipline will defeat the negative or opposing opposites. "<u>THE THOUGHT IS THE CAUSE OF IT ALL</u>".

CHAPTER TWENTY
The Internal Enemy
Man and Woman are on the Brink of Destruction

FIRST PART

Man and Woman are suppose to be GOD's greatest creation. What has gone wrong with God's prized creatures? What is the cause of Man and Woman downfall ? Some so-called experts say that**," IT'S THE ECONOMY STUPID."** Some even think that it's the lack of a good education. While a large number think that it's about Religion, and that that's the main cause of the fall of Man and Woman. Other lay the blame on bad parenting, and that if the parents wasn't born from poor families, they would have had a better chance at making a better life for themselves and the family. Lastly, a large group of US still think that we should continue to

BLAME THOSE PEOPLE FOR OUR FAILURE. You know who those other people are, right?

But, the big question still remains the same: **WHAT HAS HAPPENED TO THE MORAL AND SPIRITUALITY OF THE HUMANBEING. (MAN)?**

A very long, long time ago, a great lady, my Grandma Muriah, would often tell me that, **"IF I ACTED BAD, THE DEVIL WOULD GET ME."** And like then, I'm still asking two questions: **(1) Where is this Devil, (2) How will he get me**? She always responded by saying that He, the Devil lives in Hell, And He will burn you up if you continue to do Bad Stuff. I often wondered why she would laugh when she told us children that. Also, I wondered if what she was saying was the truth.

I'm much older now, therefore, I'm asking the same question in a different way. IS THIS DEVIL INTERNAL OR EXTERNAL, OR BOTH? If I may, I would like to suggest that this Devil may only be a force, a powerful force. And since there are negative and positive forces, the force that comes from the Devil is a negative energy that works in total opposition to the **WILL OF GOD.** Now, if this powerful energy(Force) isn't brought under control, it will turn Man and Woman, and Children into Devils. Let me make this point, remember, this force gets it's power from the **VICTIMS.** He uses **ILLUSION AND EXTORTED REALITY** to subdue us.

Therefore, when we find ourselves working in opposition to what is right(**GOD'S WAY),** we may need to check our conduct and habits. Because it may be that we are becoming **LITTLE DEVILS NOW**, and will become **BIG SERPENTS TOMORROW**). How does this force turn Man and Woman into Devils? The answer will come later, it be the Will of God....

SECOND PART

Let me use this example to explain my point. Scientists and Scholars think that the Universe operates from Mathematical expressions. In Math there are negatives and positives. The negatives will always affect the positives. **For instance: Let's say that we have a -10, and a + 5 (-10) +(+5) = -5. What's the point?** The principle is, any negative will affect the outcome, whether Mathematical or a Life Situation. **" WE MUST FIND WAYS TO DO MORE GOOD STUFF THAN THE BAD STUFF THAT WE DO". The Good must outweigh the Bad.**

Ok, let us conclude this short lesson, **"WORDS OF WISDOM FOR THE WISE"**. These aforementioned Negative Forces are called, **IMPEDIMENTS.** What are Impediments? Well, they are forces, or energies that hinder or stop the movement of people or things. For example, sometimes people are the impediment, because they will try to stop you from going further in your attempt to achieve your goal. If we listen to them, progress will be aborted. **Remember, Impediments impede and hinder movement.**

Some of these impediments are: HATE, ANGER, JEALOUSY, ENVY, INFERIORITY, AND OFCOURSE, SUPERIORITY. What about the positive forces? There are many, we will only name **a** few. They are, **LOVE, HUMBLENESS, FORGIVENESS, ATONEMENT, RECONCILIATION,** and of-course, giving a person a **SECOND CHANCE**. Humility and Love is my favorite ones, Why? Because if we can show Humbleness and Love, there isn't anything that we could not achieve, including **PEACE ON EARTH AND GOOD WILL.** The most powerful force **is LOVE.**

Lastly, if we can learn how to control the above list of forces, we will be given the keys to the **MASTERY OF SELF.** What a wonderful experience it would be if we could actually master ourselves. Once we embrace the concept of Self Mastery, we will be given the keys that will enable us to uproot the negative forces that dominate us. Please remember, that if we don't totally destroy these **KILLER NEGATIVE FORCES,** They will expand and will destroy our **THOUGHT PROCESSES. You and I are what we Think. ARE YOU READY TO START DESTROYING ALL OF THESE SICK THINKING THOUGHTS THAT IMPEDE US?** I am.

THIRD PART

In life, Man and Woman have **Needs and Wants**. Then the question becomes, **"HOW AND WHAT METHODS WILL WE USE TO ACHIEVE OUR**

ULTIMATE GOALS, (DESIRES AND WANTS)?" We must keep in mind that the **INTERNAL and EXTERNAL** enemies know what we desire, and they think that they can cause us to do anything to achieve our goals. One of the Devil's tools that he uses a lot is called**, "DECEITFUL LUST", which** is nothing but tricks and double dealing. He will make big promises to us, but he will not deliver what he has promise, unless, a bigger trick is on the way.

Now, these forces that we have been talking about will always lead Man and Woman away from **THE DIVINE POWER OF GOD.** Also, these forces have built-in negative energies that will always break-up the family. **WHY DOES SATAN TRICKS APPEAR TO ALWAYS ATTACK THE FAMILY?** Satan knows that the family is the main institution that God created that has the potential to **MAKE MAN AND WOMAN PERFECT.**

How can we escape Satan's tricks? **WE MUST PUT ON THE CLOTHING OF TRUTH**. We must start working on our **GOD GIVEN INNER POWERS, SO**

THAT OUR SPIRITUALITY WILL BECOME PURIFIED. THEREBY PREPARING US TO SEE SATAN IN HIS "EXTERNAL AND INTERNAL GARMENTS. THEN WE MUST FIND WAYS TO DESTROY THE LUSTFUL WAYS OF THE CHIEF ENEMY OF GOD.

In my conclusion, when we have submitted ourselves to God, we will gain the **WILL-POWER TO OVERCOME ANY DIFFICULTY. AFTER GAINING THIS NEW LEVEL OF WILL-POWER, WE WILL BECOME MASTERS OF OURSELVES. AND WHEN WE LEARN HOW TO MASTER OUR EMOTIONS, THEN WE WILL HAVE THE POWER TO CONTROL ALL OF THOSE "NEGATIVE URGES THAT HAS DEFEATED US.** For example, the urges of **SEX, LOVE OF MONEY, CRIME, ADULTERY, HATE, MURDER, ENVY, JEALOUSY, FORNICATION, (ALL COULD BE UNROOTED AND DESTROYED IF WE TRULY LEARN HOW TO MASTER OUR EMOTIONS. What is your opinion on how we can uproot Satan's power over Us?**

GOD'S 'Will' must be done; The Internal and External enemies are alive!!!

More the next time if it be God's Will.

Look for our next book entitled: "OVERCOMING DIFFICULTIES BY USING THE GREATEST OF INTELLIGENCE"

EPILOGUE
THE LAW AND PRINCIPLES OF THOUGHT
ORIGINAL QUOTES
BY JOHNNY X WILLIAMSON

1. All that we imagine or interpret, comes from a single thought. When you think, critically or simple, those thoughts are only new to you, because they can be as new as a new born baby. Thought is indeed the cause of it all.

2. Thinking is the business of life, when we don't think, we die.

3. Everything that we need is on the inside of us; success depends on how and when we bring the active and progressive energies out.

4. The power of thought is amazing. It's like snowflakes falling on the Earth, and if we don't protect the thought, it will melts and goes away.

5. Thought is the only principle by which we are connected and related to things that we desire, want and need.

6. Our negatives and positives are wrapped-up in our Soul's DNA. The remedy for self help is buried in our minds.

7. Go and find yourself a silent spot, then tell yourself that you are a winner, then get started making it true.

8. Thought control means developing one thought at a time. Multiple thoughts will most times confuse the primary or original thought. Thoughts are powerful, but they need to be manage thoughtfully.

9. Knowledge and Wisdom is powerful, but Discipline is the beginning stage of true greatness. You don't have to be great to get started, but you will never become great if you never get started.

10. The idea is a thought trying to be born. We will give it birth only when we think it into reality. When we fail to think, that potentially good idea will travel to a Thinker.

11. Low Self-Esteem and Hatred are connected to a Master called, 'Non-Thinker'. **THINK AND GROW.**

12. When you think that you will lose, you will; you cannot win when you think not to dare. If you are driven to win, but think that you can't, it's almost a certainty that you won't. You and I lost because we thought that we would; everything that we desire is in the world. Success begins with a human determination and Will. It's all in how we think.

13. Men and Women of greatness were once like us. Those so-called experts today were lost yesterday. They once fumbled and groped on life's highway. They were fearful of themselves, and thought that magic was man's greatest wrought. They feared to try what they did not know how to do. And they didn't know that they possessed success.

14 Why is it important to Think positive? Because, positive thinking will build in the mind's spirit cell that will act positive.

15. All the good of the past will only guide us if we embrace the idea. There is nothing new under the Sun.

16. The mind is the work station; it will work all of the rough stuff out of the original thought. It will make the idea smooth powerful. Pay attention to your mind, it talks.

17. That which is unseen always acts before the seen reacts. I think that all ideas will eventually appear, good or bad.

18. Ideas are the mother and father of all discoveries. Father and Mother working together will eventually produce the winning reality.

19 When we commit an act in the reality state. We have already committed that act in the mental state. **THE THOUGHT IS THE CAUSE OF IT ALL.**

20. I feel great knowing that Man is capable of all things, and that ideas stand in front of any action, or inaction.

21. Making the mind listen is a powerful force, but if you learn how, you are getting near the 'Mastery of self. We must tell our minds that we will win against all odds.

22. Ideas will always motivate, but make sure that you are heading in the wrong direction.

23. There is a unrecorded reason why most of us fail. What is it? Is it the lack of cash, or knowledge? No, it's because we let Sick Thoughts take advantage of Healthy Thoughts.

24. Since everything gravitates towards itself, it is critical not to think about failure in a predominate fashion. Like begets like.

25. Always make your mind see the goal, never let your mind dwell on thoughts that you don't want.

26. Fear, if not brought under control, will eventually abort the progressive movement of the individual. I call this emotion the Mind Trap. What is fear? It is **FAULTY EDUCATION APPEARING REAL.**

27. The Thought that makes us afraid is fear; the concept that makes us think inferior is fear, and failure is the direct result of fear. Low motivation is a product of fear. The way that we think is everything.

28. We must let our Subconscious and Conscious Minds enter into a covenant, one that says, We will come together as willing participants to **WIN.**

29. Ethnicity or Race is never the real cause of failure; it's always linked to "Baby Faith" that sends inferior ideas to the Mind.

30. Thought by Thought we build our fortune. And the Universe will provide the energy, Fate is the parallel of thought. Select your destiny and wait." For good things bring love and bad things bring hate and oppression.

31. The law of success has partners, and one of the main one is the law of attraction. Everything and everybody needs support.

32. If you ever need or desire to influence others, make yourself a magnet and pull them to you.

33. Never be afraid of failure or success, just try to overcome the difficulty factor.

34. Faith and Luck may work for some people, but I believe that whatever happens in life is the affect of thought.

35. Man is created in the image of God. God created Man/Woman in the divine image of Himself. Man is powerful because of his ability to Think, and then bring into reality what they thought about. What happen to this power being that God gave this original and divine power to. Is he still alive?

36. If we don't feed our Ideas they will die, and even if they locate food, which may be the wrong type, they will still die. When we provide the proper Motivational Food, which is proper thinking, the Thought will live.

37. Make yourself, convince yourself, and train yourself to believe in you. We must BE, before we can Become.

38. Stay focused, and become alive, check yourself from the inside, complaining and dreaming is for fools, either you will become a builder, or a tool. Learn to take things as they are, because you are the only real Star.

39. True mental power is when the Mind takes absolute control, and then eliminates all and any possibility of failure.

40. When people are called by their name, there is a powerful self motivation. This energy will cause them to move much quicker and willingly. When the sound comes out it creates a powerful feeling of support, togetherness and nearness.

41. Planning and Organizing are great, but the real road to success is in the land of **DESIRE.**

42. Poverty and Inferiority is like being in prison. The origin of both is connected to **THOUGHT.** There is nothing or no one who can keep you in prison if you truly desire to be free.

43. Faith and Desire working together will develop an absolute advantage in our Mind. Faith and Desire are intangibles, but real.

44. It is impossible to win if we are trapped in a 'Negative Belief System'. Eliminate the negatives and ride in on the positive.

45. Happiness and Success evolves from the same energy. The Thought did it. Remember, Desire will open the doors to happiness and success.

46. The Moment you desire anything, it becomes yours. But remember, you must lock this new desire in the heart, mind and spirit, so that it will take root.

47. You and I didn't lose because we aren't smart, we lost because we did not plant the Thought firmly in the mind.

48. Winning becomes a disease to failure. Therefore, if you want to defeat the enemy, learn how to **WIN.**

49. Mentoring is good, but Self Motivation is better. Everything that we need is in us.

50. Picking up bad habits from losers are dangerous, don't ask them, they don't know.

51. The Earth was given to us to love, but since our hearts and minds are small, we normally pollute and destroy the space. But, since we are made in a God like image, maybe our habits will reform and guide us in building a good and loving Earth.

52. The Best song hasn't been written yet, the best home hasn't been built yet, the tallest mountain hasn't been climbed yet, the fastest race hasn't been won yet.

Don't worry or fret, the chance has just begun, the race is just beginning.

53. Sometimes success isn't when we climb the biggest mountain, get the biggest house, sometimes it's the working of the smallest idea on its way to success.

54. Tomorrow is a new day that is full of issues and problems. In your mind lies either success or failure, or maybe both. It's all about how you think. **What are you thinking right NOW?**

55. Dedication, Discipline, and Durability are ladders towards success. Build the ladder, and start moving towards the starting line.

56. The enemy of success is fear, and he is powerful and smart. Therefore, if you are to overcome him, you must use your smarts powerfully.

57. Tune in to God and live, tune in to yourself and grow, and if you critique and examine yourself passionately, you will find the hidden Keys to Success.

58. Sometimes when we speak, our words project wisdom. Sometimes we can project the same wisdom and energy by staying silent and still.

59. The great benefit of staying silent sometimes is that if you are not talking, then perhaps you may-be listening.

60. Secrets always stimulate the mind, ideas do the same. Remember, Locking your thoughts in the mind will give you added Mind power.

61. Man/Woman has yet to discover their true potential. Our real power is buried in a Sea of disbelief and fear. Our real greatness is directly connected to the divine spirit God.

62. Never depend on Faith alone. You must mix faith with work, plus a little bit of desire. Then you are ready to successfully bake the cake of success.

63. We can make our destiny as bright as the sunlight, or we can let the dark shadow of fear destroy our great potential. We must move against those old Spirit Destroyers. Because they are the cause of the Negative Thoughts Buildups.

64. The race is never won in the beginning. Everything has three dimensions, a starting point, the middle action, and of course the thrilling and motivating End.

65. Faith is unseen yet exceedingly powerful. It is intangible, invisible, and some say mysterious. But, there isn't anything under the sun that can move the impossible like faith can. I think that Faith is connected to the Nature of God.

66. There is nothing on Earth that does not belong to You and I, Nothing. Everything on our planet is a gift from God to us.

67. If our brilliant minds built the Pyramids, and I know that they did. The question today is, What is our minds working on today? Why is the Ghetto still there?

ABOUT THE AUTHOR

Johnny X Williamson's powerful book **THE THOUGHT IS THE CAUSE OF IT ALL** references the inner workings of the human mind, that create reality (both success and failure) in our personal life, family and community. It is a definitive and superb masterpiece of supreme insight for any person seeking clarity about their life direction and purpose.